T0129152

STONE IN A SLING

STONE IN A SLING

A Soldier's Journey

Major (Ret.) Scott A. Meehan

iUniverse LLC
Bloomington

STONE IN A SLING
A Soldier's Journey

iUniverse books may be ordered through booksellers or by contacting:

iUniverse LLC
1663 Liberty Drive
Bloomington, IN 47403
www.iuniverse.com
1-800-Authors (1-800-288-4677)

ISBN: 978-1-4759-9487-2 (sc)
ISBN: 978-1-4759-9488-9 (ebk)

Library of Congress Control Number: 2013910831

Printed in the United States of America

iUniverse rev. date: 06/24/2013

CONTENTS

Preface..ix
Introduction: Baghdad, Iraq March 2006..xi

Part 1:   The Cold War..1
Chapter 1   Bogota, Colombia August 1976..............................3
Chapter 2   "Be All You Can Be" Fort Benning,
                 Georgia August 1980 17
Chapter 3   Southern Pines, North Carolina
                 September 1980..24
Chapter 4   Fort Bragg, North Carolina 1980 33
Chapter 5   The "Pit" and the Phone Booth Fort
                 Sam Houston, Texas 1981......................................38
Chapter 6   Amazon Emeralds March 1981................................43
Chapter 7   Marriage Salem, Virginia October 1981..................52
Chapter 8   Behind the Wall East and West Berlin
                 1984-1987 58

Part 2:   Commissioned, and the War on Terror 81
Chapter 9   Desert Storm Riyadh, Saudi Arabia
                 January 1991 83
Chapter 10   Kibrit Enemy Prisoner of War (EPW)
                 Camp Saudi Arabian Desert March 1991 100
Chapter 11   Defense Acquisitions Orlando, Florida
                 1998-2002..112
Chapter 12   Déjà Vu Riyadh, Saudi Arabia
                 June-September 2003..129
Chapter 13   Operation Iraqi Freedom (OIF)
                 Camp Anaconda, Balad, Iraq 2003-2004................133

Chapter 14   One More Mission The Green Zone
              Baghdad, Iraq 2005 160
Chapter 15   The End of the Journey..169
Chapter 16   Final Word Baghdad, Iraq—2006-2007..................179

References..191

To my grandmother, Hilda Larrimore Meehan, for her spiritual inspiration and heritage. She went to heaven in April 2012, at age 102.

Hilda Larrimore Meehan in 1929

PREFACE

This book began in 2007 following the end of my last deployment to Iraq as a contractor. The idea behind *Stone in a Sling* is one based on memories and lessons learned from a soldier's perspective. It contains a unique introspective view of a soldier's life during the Cold War, Desert Storm, and the War on Terror. Face-to-face encounters included enemies and allies alike, such as a Soviet KGB officer, a Saudi prince, Iraqi Sunni, Shi'a, Kurds, and Colombian terrorists. Developed relationships with the Iraqi people led to the capture of Saddam Hussein.

I wanted something in writing for my grandmother, an avid reader, before her time with us here would be absent. She was ninety-seven at the time of this book's first publication. Our family was able to celebrate her one hundredth birthday in 2010. In April 2012, Hilda went to heaven. She had the opportunity to read my book before she departed.

I would like to recognize my wife of thirty-one years, Trena. I cannot even imagine what my journey would have been like without her. She has stood by me through thick and thin.

My adult "children" Aaron and Jacquelyn (Jacquie). I am proud of you both.

My son-in-law, Chris Currie, an infantry trooper with the Florida National Guard.

My new grandson, Jaden Allen Curie (eighteen months).

My parents, Al and Carole. Both of you are an inspiration with your faithful dedication throughout the years.

My brother, Russ, and his family. He certainly can identify to our earlier journeys together.

Trena's family: her parents, three sisters, and brother-in-law, Rev. Jesse Bass, and his family.

Finally, to all the men and women in uniform along with their husbands, wives, children, grandchildren, parents, and grandparents. God Bless all of you!

Scott Allan Meehan
USA, Major (Ret.)

Introduction

Baghdad, Iraq
March 2006

Reaching into his bag and taking out a stone, he slung it and
struck the Philistine on the forehead.
—1 Samuel 17:49 (NIV)

The interior of the Blackhawk helicopter was dark except for
the pilot and copilot's glowing control panel. The door gunners
scanned the shadows below. Night observation devices (NODS)
were attached to their helmets and lowered over their eyes, emitting
a fluorescent glow against the black night.

Thawap, thawap, thawap. The droning sound of the rotor blades
seemed deafening as we cruised above the city lights and streets of
Baghdad. Tiny green and blue lights glared eerily back from the
instrument panel like watchful eyes. The two door gunners, one
on each side of the chopper, sat behind their .249-caliber machine
guns with their hands holding on, protected by leather suede gloves.
They searched for anything out of place, such as the silhouetted
shape of a rocket-propelled grenade (RPG) tube aiming skyward.

I sat toward the tail, facing the front, in a row of four passengers
packed in tightly, knee-to-knee, with duffle bags piled to the top on
our laps. Across from us sat two other soldiers and a pair of civilian
contractors. I was wedged between two men wearing army combat
uniforms, or ACUs, beneath their flak vests, and it struck me that
I was the odd one, wearing civilian attire in a combat zone for the
first time.

The high-pitched whining of the rotors cutting through the
thick night air was still loud, even with our yellow-foamed earplugs

jammed in our ears. For me, the noise alternated from being a nerve-racking distraction to a hypnotic entrancement that was causing drowsiness. Whenever the aircraft took a sudden bounce I continued to breathe steadily; the tremors were common and no cause for panic. I looked at the sleeping men around me with their heads bobbing limply back and forth with each bump.

We were on a northeastern course from Camp Victory, on the southwest side of Baghdad, to Forward Operating Base (FOB) Warhorse, which was just outside of Baqouba. The plan was to make a pit stop there before turning northwest across the desert to our final destination at Camp Speicher, near Tikrit. Camp Speicher would be my new home base, where I was to conduct operations there for at least a year for my new employer—my first full-time civilian job since 1980.

I glanced at my watch—1:00 a.m. We were over the Shi'a section of the city, considered hostile territory. *What wasn't in Iraq?* I wondered. My eyelids drooped heavily, and I thought back to my other two deployments to Iraq as an army officer. *Why had I allowed myself to return to this God-forsaken place; the money?* Made good sense to me at the time. The pay would certainly be more than I ever made!

Serving at Camp Anaconda from 2003 to 2004 was one of the longest years of my life. I swore to myself and anyone who would listen that I'd never go back to Iraq. And yet, just a year later, I headed to the Green Zone in Baghdad. That time, I had vowed, would be the final time. I fully intended to come home to my family and retire. Here I was, for the third time.

My eyes opened to the flickering lights out the window. Baghdad's sprawling city faded and brightened with varying degrees of intensity below us. *Baghdad.* Sighing, I let my eyes close again. *Lord, did I hear you right on this one?*

Leaving my wife, Trena, was never easy no matter how many times I left. The first time was in 1991, and the pain was crushing. I kept a journal where I could unload my feelings and fears about leaving her and my two children—ages six and eight. I was unaware of what was in store for me when heading to Saudi Arabia to face the fourth largest army in the world at the time. I never realized, until later, what it was like for Trena to kiss a husband good-bye and not know if he would ever return.

Years later, during Operation Iraqi Freedom, the kids were fully grown and moving forward with their own lives. I thought that leaving would have been easier, but the emptiness remained. I still thought about all missed opportunities of being there for my family.

Going back to Iraq after retirement had not been in the original plan. I was thinking more in line with lying in a hammock strung up between two palm trees, watching the waves of the sea and setting sun, with a cool drink and protruding curved straw. But it was impossible to ignore the salary I was offered. Trena and I discussed the advantages and disadvantages of accepting the job offer, and, in the end, it was a simple matter of economics and following what we believed to be God's will for us.

Bang! My eyes snapped open. Heads jerked up around me. A loud crash erupted on the pilot's side of the helicopter! In seconds, the door gunners swung into firing posture.

A bright orange and white light burst with a blinding flash around us on the left side, contrasting brilliantly against the black sky. For a brief second, the interior of the chopper lit up like a strobe light. The soldiers' faces around were clear as day.

Intense heat licked my face and arms, and I gripped my seat firmly as the Blackhawk dove sharply to the right. The streetlights grew closer to the window, and the mud-walled dwellings loomed larger and larger.

Danger was not new to me, but the fear still permeated my thoughts. *Would I survive this one as I did in the bombing in Colombia? What if I survive the crash and am taken captive? Will the Shia's treat me with the same courtesy as the Soviets had in Berlin?* My head swirled fast, as if I was spinning on a high-speed roller coaster, too fast to think coherently. Many times I had met the enemy, face-to-face.

PART 1

THE COLD WAR

CHAPTER 1

BOGOTA, COLOMBIA
AUGUST 1976

The horrific blasting sound jolted me wide awake in seconds. My eyes struggled to focus in the darkness of the small, simple, white room on the second floor of the apartment. In the twin bed against the wall, I wondered how a noise in my dreams could have had such an effect. I shrugged it off sleepily, desiring to find sound sleep back in the rack beneath the covers.

While attempting my reentry into dreamland, I began hearing jumbled sounds of people outside my door. I perked up and listened intently, trying to hear what was being said. When I heard the word, Fire! I reacted. It started with a burst of motion starting with my feet hitting the floor, blue jeans zipped around my waist, shirt flung over my head, boots shoved onto my feet, and my hand on the doorknob, all in a matter of seconds! I fumbled for the lock and, once found, stumbled into the hallway. Chaos surrounded me. I got up so fast that my blood rushed to my head, causing dizziness. Feeling faint, I leaned against the wall and wondered if my time was up.

"Are you all right?" I heard Bobby ask. "You don't look so good." His mouth, usually open in loud laughter, was a tight, thin line.

"Yeah, give me a minute." I breathed in deeply, steadying myself. "What's going on?"

Bobby was a high school classmate at our Christian mission base in Lomalinda. "I heard that a bomb just went off downstairs!"

I blinked once, confused. "What the . . . ?" I couldn't wrap my mind around what he'd just said.

Other Christian missionaries assigned to the Colombian branch were milling about—dazed—not sure of how to react or how to comprehend the unfolding events. Bobby and I started toward the stairs that led down to the first floor of the three-story complex—ground zero—at least according to the bits of information we'd heard upstairs. As we descended the stairs with caution, the walls from the first-floor offices were in a heap of rubble.

At the bottom of the stairway a twisted pile of broken, splintered wood blocked our path. The front, once enclosed by a metal entrance door and two-car garage door, and separated by a brick partition, was now fully exposed to the street. A gaping hole across the building front opened to the gathering Colombian crowd in the glass-shattered streets, staring at the carnage before them. A young American girl, maybe thirteen or fourteen, stood in terror, her wide blue eyes piercing through her strands of hair, gazed at the carnage before her. She clutched a blanket and pillow and seemed to be in shock.

An older teenage girl stood a few feet away in conversation with a young guy. Her light brown hair hung to her shoulders, and she wore wire-rimmed glasses. Also present was a muscular guy in jeans, leather jacket, and black cowboy boots. Neither Bobby nor I recognized any of them. We began walking toward them, and as they saw our approach, they turned to greet us. The male was stocky and muscular with long, dark, curly hair.

"Hi, I'm Doug Kindberg," the big guy said right away, in a low voice that told me I'd underestimated his age.

The brunette smiled openly. "And I'm his sister, Kathy."

"Scott Meehan," I countered.

"I'm Bobby Wheeler," Bobby chimed in beside me, sounding a little more like the bold, outgoing Bobby that I knew.

"That's our younger sister, Virginia," Kathy continued, nodding her head in the direction of the young girl with the raven hair and blanket.

"What happened?" Bobby asked.

"We just arrived here tonight, from Peru. We pulled into the driveway and were unloading our baggage when my dad walked over to the front door and picked up a small white package. He said, 'What's this, a bomb or something?'"

Kathy added quickly. "Then Bill yelled, 'Yes, yes, it is a bomb; it's a bomb!'"

"So our dad dropped the box and yelled, 'Run. Run for your lives!' I hightailed it down the street and then, *boom!*"

"I hid behind the car!" Kathy added.

I stared at them in disbelief. "Nobody was hurt?"

"Nobody out here," Kathy continued.

I imagined the scene, and what might've happened had Bill not been there to identify the package. I scanned the crowd for Bill. Bill Nyman was the liaison in Bogota who had picked up the Kindberg family from the airport and brought them to the apartment complex. Miraculously, nobody was injured inside or outside of the complex, but the damage was extensive.

I looked down the street toward the east and west along the rows of brick complexes; all of the windows on both sides of the street were blown out. Glass covered the road. I understood at once that our street, Calle 42, near the University in Barrio Soledad, had changed that day.

Emergency crews continued to swarm the area. Crowds stood in packs, as if they'd be safer in numbers. Dick Inlow, the apartment manager, stopped when he saw us. "The police said that our God must have been with all of us tonight because this type of bomb was set to trigger immediately upon pickup. Also, other bombs went off around the city, more powerful than this one." His eyes were far off, as if his mind was somewhere else. Later, he'd tell me about bolting awake, thinking the water heater had exploded—about the shattered glass beneath his bare feet.

"DAS is saying that it's the work of the M-19." With that, Dick kept going, toward the charred building. I let his response sink in. The M-19 was the leftist organization known in Colombia as the Movimiento 19 de Abril, whose origins could be traced back to the alleged fraudulent presidential elections of April, 19, 1970. Their ideology was a mixture of populism and nationalistic evolutionary socialism, widespread in the 1970s. They also didn't think too kindly of us, whom they referred to as gringos.

We eventually exhausted our insight of the evening-turned-to-morning events, and out of the desire for distraction as much as actual interest, we moved on to other topics. As the others around me talked, I reflected on the past twenty-four hours.

For me, the tumultuous evening began two days before at our mission base, Lomalinda. The base was surrounded by a combination of dry forest, grasslands, rivers, lakes, and rolling hills. Marcia, my girlfriend, had broken things off, just as I was about to board the single-engine aircraft bound for Bogota, a Helio Courier, the same type of plane my dad flew for the mission. I remembered the look on her face and the shortness of her speech, and it surprised me again, painfully, how easy it'd seemed for her to end it.

Marcia had just returned from Bogota with her best friend, Anita, the very morning that I was leaving for Bogota. We met briefly at the base hangar as she deplaned, and I boarded. Our relationship had been shaky for weeks, and she had already informed me before her trip that she would be considering our future. I was hoping that she'd chosen to remain with me, but I was uncertain. My stomach clenched as I approached her.

"Hi, Marcia," I said, smiling nervously. I took in her face carefully, studying its curves and angles. Although she was three years my junior, the American missionary girl had won me over easily, and had made my remaining months in Colombia sweeter.

"Hi," she muttered, tucking a strand of dark hair behind her ear. She avoided my gaze, and it hit me immediately that this was not going to end in my favor.

"I guess you made your decision." My smile vanished abruptly.

"Yes," she said matter-of-factly. "It's just not going to work out. I've decided to move on." Just like that. "Look, we can talk about this when you get back."

She was right; the pilot was ready to make a quick turnaround, so I shuffled dejectedly toward the plane. The plane lifted into the Colombian blue sky, over the vast rolling plains and tropical grasslands in the Orinoco River basin. Everything I'd thought I wanted remained on the ground. I watched out the window as the hangar got smaller and smaller until finally disappearing.

The flight course was set for the cowboy town of Villavicencio, the capital of Meta, a province in the Llanos, open, grassy plains, of Colombia. This was as far as the Helio would take us before we would exchange our plane ride for a wild taxi adventure over the Andean mountains. This long, winding trip now seemed like nothing more than a cage for my thoughts and me.

I stared out the small window, pondering her words. Below me were patches of lakes, huts, ranch style homes, and smoke patches as the llanos stretched across eastern Colombia and southern Venezuela. Surrounding the llanos was the Andean Mountains to the west, the Venezuelan Atlantic coast to the north, and the Amazon jungle to the south. The caiman, a crocodile mix, lived in the region, along with the capybara, the largest rodent in the world, and the anaconda, the largest boa in the world. Just weeks before, a local rancher had lassoed a seventeen-and-a-half-foot anaconda that had tried to swallow one of his cattle! And yet, all of the exotic beauty and adventure was lost on me. I wanted none of it.

Finally, the plane landed in Villavicencio, and six of us climbed into a Nissan blazer-type cab to begin our trip up the mountain. We made a stop midway, and as soon as I got out, the dry air chilled me. This was certainly a stark contrast to the tropic humidity of the llanos. The cab driver ate his steak and rice while I hunched my shoulders, adjusted my denim jacket, and waited glumly, oblivious to the spectacular mountain scenery.

The cab driver ushered us back into the cab, and we continued on our way. Hours dragged on, and, soon enough, my thoughts were jolted to the present by commotion on the street as we descended the mountain into the city of Bogotá. Bogotá was an amazing sight from the mountaintop. Towering buildings stood clustered together with colonial style cathedrals and spread north as far as the eye could see. Nestled high in the Andes, 8,646 feet above sea level, the ride from Villavicencio was a steady uphill climb before the final descent.

Broken-down shacks located in the south zone gradually gave way to larger structures, growing taller by the mile. Typical Colombian salsa music blared from storefronts, mingling with the chaotic noises of wild traffic patterns, which were virtually nonexistent. Ever present were thieves, beggars, street kids, drug dealers, and street vendors peddling emeralds. Mixed with these seedier types were the weary, hardworking fathers and struggling mothers clutching their youngsters by the hand, grandmothers in black shawls shuffling along, and smartly dressed secretaries and suave young businessmen. Sometimes it was difficult to make the distinction between up-and-coming businessmen and the not so honest because the thieves often dressed in business suits, and the honest could not afford anything better than worn-out clothing.

Despite my inner bleakness, I couldn't help but notice an uncharacteristically beautiful sunset, which left hues of purple, red, and pink just above the plateau. Numerous high-rise buildings could be seen clearly in the valley, indicating that a clean rain had washed the ever-present pollution from the usually hazy sky. I enjoyed the cool mountain breeze hitting me in the face from the open window, but I was careful to keep alert for opportunities that endorsed vanishing wristwatches.

I took in the busy city life, which afforded a slight reprieve from my thoughts of Marcia. Soon, the familiar neighborhood around Caracas 50 appeared, and in a short time the taxi pulled into the driveway in front of the three-story apartment building located along a row of solid concrete, gray and reddish brick buildings. The mission's group house was located on Calle 42 near the University in Barrio Soledad. The numbers 24-32 were engraved in the cement above the thick metal door.

As we spilled out of the cab, everyone notably raised their arms and stretched, reaching for the sky. Usual traffic continued to whip by in front of the mission house with the occasional screech of brakes, the honking of a horn, and the accompanying yelling in Spanish. Although the sun was setting, the foot traffic along the sidewalk was still congested as people rushed about finishing their day's work and headed home.

There wasn't much for me to do, no plans, none of my friends to hang out with at the time. It was just me, a few other missionaries, most with younger kids, and my reflections. Nightfall came soon enough, and before I ascended the stairs to bed down for the night on the second floor of the complex, I paused at the front door of the apartment complex after a long walk.

Marcia and I had frequently ridden together on my Honda 90 motorcycle, the most common mode of transportation on the base. She would be on the back, her dark chestnut hair streaming back like flowing waves, laughing, clinging on for dear life whenever we cleared the top of a hill with both wheels off the ground after revving the throttle at full speed. The beautiful view of the Serrania de La Macarena loomed ahead whenever we streamed into the wind facing the western sunset. The multicolored evening hues of the mountain range protruding west of the base had been a romantic backdrop for our times together. Experiencing those times together was about to come to an end, and I was helpless to stop it.

Emotionally, a turbulent disturbance was already in full force within me, and now, combined with this life-threatening explosive experience, I felt that it wouldn't take much more to send me over the edge. Although I was not targeted specifically, I sure took it personally. My senior year had ended well but was quickly taking a drastic turn for the worse, and I was just months away from returning to the United States and pursuing my future in the workforce or college.

Seventeen years prior to this moment, in 1958, I entered the world in the city of Baltimore, two months before the Colts brought the championship there for the first time. My parents were not wealthy by any stretch of the imagination. They had married when both were at the tender age of eighteen.

My mother came from a German-Finnish heritage on the east side of town. My father, a young, ambitious man, came from the English-Irish line of Meehans, Harringtons, and Larrimores. Although they met in church, my grandmother was not keen in the least on such a young marriage. Thick tension dominated the atmosphere early at my grandparents' two-story house on Rolling Road.

Three years after my birth, my brother, Russ, came into the world. The four of us moved from my grandparents' home and into an apartment on the north side of town. Here, my father would start his new career as a Baltimore County police officer stationed in Towson.

As we grew older, Russ and I enjoyed the life of most young boys—getting into mischief, playing whiffle ball, going to baseball games, and the fun that accompanies youth. Church on Sunday morning was a given whether we liked it or not. We actually did like it when one of the men of the church along with his son entertained all of us youngsters with magic tricks. Our trips to Dundalk, on the east side, were a bit more exciting because we could team with our uncle Duane and find interesting activities not otherwise privy to our experience at home.

Sometime after living in the small apartments, we moved into a newly bought house in Woodlawn where my father was transferred. The neighborhood was typically nice by '60s standards—mowed lawns, school buses, the milkman, Good Humor man, and the like. This was where I began the first grade. It was also during that time when *Combat*, with Vic Morrow, became one of my favorite TV shows. I first wanted to be a soldier because of this series. Of course, it's easy to imagine being a soldier from the living room floor far removed from feeling any pain produced by bullet wounds. It was equally easy to imagine I would also live forever.

However, life and death became a subject one afternoon when vacationing in Atlantic City, New Jersey, with many family members. I was at the edge of one of the piers when my mother pointed out some whales over the horizon. Fascinated by their majestic flow and large, black, sleek appearance while shooting white jets of water into the deep blue sky, I asked my mom a question, and her response caused me great distress.

"Mom," I began, "will they live forever?"

I was stricken with sadness by her answer. "No, honey, nothing lives forever."

It took me a couple of seconds to allow her words to sink in. "Nothing, not even me?"

"Well, only if you believe in Jesus as God's Son, then when you do die, you can live forever in heaven," she informed me. This whole revelation caused me great concern, and my brain was swimming with questions. I heard basically the same thing from a Sunday school teacher, but she had added that Jesus loved the whole world, even the bad guys.

Toward the end of second grade, Russ and I learned that we were moving—not only from Woodlawn but also from Baltimore altogether. My father, after listening to a missionary from Colombia speak at our church who told the story of five missionary jungle pilots that were martyred in the Amazon jungles of Ecuador, made a major life correction choice. He chose to step into the gap and become a missionary pilot and began to make arrangements to resign from the Baltimore County Police Department.

This journey began with a move to Chicago, Illinois, the city where the Moody Bible Institute was located, ironically, in a place where the spotlight of the Playboy building could be seen clearly on any given night. Moody Bible Institute had the only combination of Bible courses and aviation program at the time. My father's new ambition and dream began with what many would consider to be a sacrifice.

Moving in such fashion was a drastic change for family members on both sides of the harbor. Though not fully understanding this rash decision, over time they all came to accept it and pledged their support in every way. My mother, ever faithful, may have had her misgivings, but Russ and I would never have known it if she had.

Attending school in Chicago was certainly different than the suburban Baltimore County one I had previously attended. Walking the two city blocks of Chicago to and from Nettle horse Elementary twice a day should have normally carried a challenge of survival. However, when we moved into the new neighborhood, Russ and I, not knowing any better, did not retreat to our apartment like the others did when the Puerto Rican kids came around to play ball. As a result, we established our first cross-cultural friendships. Better yet, we didn't have to worry about getting beat up by some psychopathic kid at school because our new friends provided a nice protection plan.

Despite the safety of such a setup, my parents found it necessary to send Russ and me to a private Christian school the following year. Although I learned a lot more about the Bible than ever, the trip to and from school was in a station wagon filled with about seven or eight other kids. And, of course, there was always going to be one or two of them who acted psychopathic. Unfortunately, I was without my protection plan and wound up on the receiving end of a beating on several occasions.

Relief from these beatings came when my father finally finished his Bible college training and then the flight portion ensued. This meant further moves. Because of the nature of his training, we found ourselves living in such places as Johnson City, Tennessee; Waxhaw, North Carolina; Chiapas, Mexico; Santa Ana, California; and San Jose, Costa Rica; all within the next five years. Our journeys across the map weaved back and forth like a spider's web.

The coolest home we lived in was one made of sticks and equipped with a homemade mud stove. This was a family team effort accomplished in the jungles of southern Mexico. Food was rationed, and the milk was powdered. At least our home made of sticks had a front view of the most crystal-clear lakes I have ever seen.

When we finally reached our final destination, the mission field assignment, I was in tenth grade and Russ was in the seventh. We arrived in Bogota, Colombia, in the summer of '73 and then traveled farther into the interior, where the base was located. Home would be the land of gold, emeralds, coffee, and cocaine. Several hundred other missionary families were also located at the base, including girls my age, with some of whom I would share plenty of time.

When graduation approached two years later, my emotions were mixed. I envisioned the adventure, enjoyment, diversion, and all the pleasures that American society had to offer. Yet, at the same time, I had to face reality that included searching for and finding a job, or even possibly furthering my education in a college. I did not feel ready for college.

I read a verse from Philippians in the Bible saying not to worry about anything, which contradicted my true feelings, and I was to pray about everything. I eventually learned to put this concept into practice. Soon afterward, my parents left for the United States along with my brother. I had the privilege of hanging back a bit longer and finishing some courses that I hadn't been able to finish because they had arrived late in the school year.

Bogota—August 1976

All of my childhood thoughts and future concerns almost came to an abrupt halt on this night in Bogota. I contemplated many aspects of life before this night, but after the explosion, I thought hard about the basics of living.

Dawn crept up slowly while people still milled about the streets. Most of them went on home to begin another day. The air was brisk and windy, and the clouds moved along rapidly as if trying to reach a destination by a certain time. Remnants of a violent, dark night glistened gold on the Bogota streets from the rising sun. Ironically, this visual gave me a renewed sense of hope to move forward and pick up the pieces of what could have been a shattered life.

A Nissan cab arrived on schedule to pick up the small group of us traveling back to the mission base of operations. Wondering what had transpired, the driver's expression was one of hesitant horror. We, along with the police, assured him that everything was under control and that it would be safe for him to take us to our destination. All of us were in a hurry to leave, and it didn't take long to convince the cabbie to depart.

One month after the bombing incident, I was headed back to Bogota for my monthly orthodontist appointment. I was leery about returning to the scene of destruction but was informed that there were twenty-four-hour guards patrolling the complex, and there was no need to worry.

This trip would only be for two nights anyway, so that was time enough to take care of business and then get out of Dodge. On my second night there, I went to the movies with several other missionary kids (MKs), who happened to be in Bogota for one reason or another. Janet, a girl two years younger than me, with long, wavy blond hair and blue eyes hidden behind wire-rimmed glasses, was there along with her mother, brother, and three other girls. The superior number of girls present meant I was outvoted as to what we saw at the cinema, and it turned out to be *The Sound of Music*.

To me, a James Bond fan, the ending of the movie was the best part as I sat through and endured. The highlight of the evening was about to come, and I was looking forward to a steak sandwich at a Steak 'n Shake type of place called Crème Helado. Rather than hailing a cab or waiting for an overcrowded bus, we decided to walk the several blocks to the restaurant as twilight settled over the Andean plateau.

As we walked, joked, laughed, and exchanged stories, including my exciting review of the movie, conversation quickly turned to the bombing incident that had taken place the previous month, a topic I would well have rather avoided. The chaotic scene of that evening began playing in my mind all over again—the crowds of people standing around in shock, the streets strewn with glass, and the apartment building standing open to the world with a gaping hole as if the building was trying to yell for help.

I found myself detached from the rest of the group as they continued forward full of conversation. My feet kept moving, but my pace had slowed so that I began drifting farther back from the pack. Inner turmoil was taking hold of me now. Mentally isolated from the rest of the group, I was feeling tormented by my own personal demons. At this particular moment, the main antagonist was fear.

"Hey, Scott, are you coming?" Janet asked. The rest of the group stopped and turned around to face me.

"Yeah, keep going. I'll catch up," I managed to say.

"Are you all right?" Janet's mother asked me.

"Yes, I'm fine. Go ahead; I'll be right behind you," I answered.

"Okay," one of them answered; I wasn't sure who. They turned around and continued walking, every now and then peering over their shoulders to see if I was still behind them.

I wrestled with this unrelenting opponent—fear—who, with the mere recollection of an event now a month in the past, had shown me how extremely vulnerable I was to the world's elements. Life, which was fast becoming complicated enough with my breakup, graduation, and the decisions I would have to make when I returned to the United States the next month, became more unsettling than I could ever have imagined.

"A bomb!" I exclaimed chokingly to myself. "How close was I to a violent death that night?" The realization came at me like never before. Nothing like this should ever happen to anyone. I didn't know how to act or what to do; I was helpless.

My only relief since the incident had come about through the moments that I had set aside to converse with God. I did this with the Bible opened to the book of Psalms. For some reason, I could relate to David's words during the moments of his inner conflict. I convinced myself that God was still pleased with me. "You have preserved my life because I am innocent" (Psalm 41:12—New Living Translation).

Still tagging behind the small group, I was feeling anxious, and I could feel, inside, a swelling of fear. Sweat began pouring down both sides of my smooth, baby face. Looking quickly to my right and then left, I saw nothing, further confirming my paranoia. But I felt for sure that someone or something was there. *But where? But what?* I could feel my eyelids flutter. I looked again quickly behind me. *Still nothing.*

"What's wrong with me?" I wanted to scream.

Then, without warning, I felt an actual invisible force of a heavy weight pressed down upon my shoulders, trying to crush me to the ground. I had to stop walking. Like being stuck in a dream, I wanted to yell for help, but no words escaped my mouth. Besides, I wondered, what would have been the purpose to yell since nothing could be seen around me? The whole scene was surreal.

Like a flashing neon sign, the words from Psalm 23:4 came to me clear as a picture in my mind so I blurted the words out, "When I walk through the valley of the shadow of death, I will not be afraid, because you are there with me, your rod and staff comforting me."

Immediately, the plunging grip weighing on my shoulders left me completely. Not only had the feeling vanished, it was replaced entirely by an overwhelming sense of peace. The dark streets of Bogotá seemed to have lit up around me. This paranormal event allowed me to smile while wondering at the same time what had just transpired. One thing I knew for certain, I had just, and perhaps with the help of an unseen angel, conquered my fears.

I picked up my pace, wanting to catch up with the rest of the MKs, who were probably guessing that I was being a teenage boy who needed some time to myself. Crème Helado appeared, and as we entered the restaurant, the Colombian waiter sat the seven of us at a table next to an open hearth, facing the busy main street out front.

After ordering my usual steak sandwich, fries, and vanilla milkshake, I caught sight out of the window of the commonly seen street kids, referred to by the locals as *gamines*. Another name attributed to them, one that was disheartening, was "throwaway children." These young Colombian boys varied in age, and I could see them running in and out of their makeshift cardboard dwellings located on the grassy median between the busy avenidas. Some of the older ones ran up to patrons who were either getting into their parked cars or exiting them in the hope of being there in time to open or close their car doors and earn a token for their labors. As I waited for my food, my eyes became riveted to the open flames in the stone fireplace behind our table.

What had just taken place back there? I didn't know how I would ever explain it, an angel coming to my rescue and knocking out a demonic force maybe? Despite my inability to adequately explain what had taken place, I did know that something special had transpired. My thoughts moved forward as I continued gazing into the flames. I was ready to begin my stateside journey wherever it would take me.

CHAPTER 2

"BE ALL YOU CAN BE"
FORT BENNING, GEORGIA
AUGUST 1980

Sweat dripped down my face like a waterfall in the hundred-degree heat. The brutal Georgian humidity caused our drenched T-shirts to stick to our bodies. This was just a small price to pay for the privilege of becoming a US Army paratrooper. During "Ground Week," more than one hundred of us, in several different groups, were marched over to the outdoor overhead showers by the cadre. There, we would lie down on a hot concrete slab, much like a wide driveway, and then roll across the cement like bowling balls in our olive drab pants and sweat-stained white T-shirts. Several overhead pipes, evenly spaced in rows, sprayed showers of water down upon us, soaking our bodies, and what was once our previously inspected, highly spit-shined boots.

Ah, what a relief the cool spray of water was to our physical need for hydration. But the moment of pleasure ended too quickly. Little time passed before our bodies absorbed the liquid like a sponge, and the blazing sun zapped the moisture back away from us. Today, however, training was a priority, and the outdoor shower would have to wait for another hour or so. During our first full week of training, we learned to exit from a door position by jumping out of a thirty-four-foot tower while being hooked up to a bungee cord. The cord slid down a long wire that extended to the far end of the field, where other soldiers waited to catch those who had just jumped.

Other drills focused us on keeping our feet together, evaluated by sliding down a T-bar and letting go when the cadre, affectionately called "black-hats," told us to drop-fall to the ground quickly to administer push-ups. They would critique our landing, ensuring that our feet were together, and we fell on the correct four points of contact. Throughout the first week, no matter where I looked across the field, there were trainees scattered in every direction doing push-ups for one infraction or another, all under the gentle watch care of the black hat that stood over them.

Airborne School was an adventure that I hoped would play a large part in my attempt to become a man. Only four months prior to being in this sweat-hole, I had entered the army at Fort Leonard Wood, Missouri. Prior to that moment of enlistment, I had spent four years wandering throughout the United States, including a year at a small college, looking for the answer to what I should do with my life. Everything seemed to end in disappointment or failure, all factors that led me to attempt to become one of America's elite fighting men.

Two weeks after the finish of ground zero, and four years after I first began my search for direction for my life, I was walking out the door of a flying C-141 jet aircraft. I recall the experience quite vividly; the exhilarating memory of the event remains clear even to this day.

I still remember the emotions I felt on the night before the big day of the jump. I went for a walk until I spotted a log lying at the edge of some woods. Sitting down, and remembering a soldier at Fort Sam Houston, Texas, who was always lifting a small New Testament out of his shirt pocket during breaks, I reached for my little green issued Bible.

Opening its tiny pages, I flipped to the words, "Trust in the Lord with all your heart and don't lean on your own understanding. In all your ways acknowledge Him and He will direct your paths" (Proverbs 3:5-6). Those words were a sense of comfort to me that evening, and I was as ready as ever to jump from an aircraft while in flight.

The big day of my first jump began in a large open hangar with wooden tables attached side-by-side, room enough for all the jump-gear that a couple of hundred soon-to-be airborne soldiers would need. Once the process of suiting up was complete—a carefully executed partnership process—I stepped behind the soldier in front of me as we walked single file out onto the tarmac toward the three awaiting aircraft. Several other lines of soldiers inched their way toward the lumbering birds as well.

Here we were, long lines of future paratroopers dressed in olive drab uniforms with a bright yellow static line running down our backs from the packed chute. As we headed to the open end of the aircraft, where ramps stretched out before us, the scene reminded me of exotic caterpillars crawling toward their predetermined destination. One by one the lines split apart toward one of the three designated planes, a C-130 and a C-123, both propeller planes, and a C-141 jetliner. I wasn't sure how to react to the fact that I was in the line heading toward the jet. Then, methodically, each iron bird engulfed the prodding green and yellow line like a bird with a wide open mouth swallowing a worm.

I made my way up the ramp behind the others and then stumbled to the red-strapped jump seats situated along the skin of the aircraft and facing toward the middle. What made matters more complicated was the fact that there were also more jump seats placed at the center of the aircraft facing us. This uncomfortable squeeze forced bulkily packed soldiers to cramp together, face-to-face and knee to knee as we all made a desperate attempt to sit down like normal people. The word sardines came to mind.

Joining the army was not a planned event for me. But banging around the United States for four years after graduating high school and then spending a year at an expensive private college wasn't working for me. In fact, nothing seemed to be. My grades in college dictated that I needed to find some type of focus in my life. But what? It was my dad, the missionary pilot, who decided to help me along by visiting the marine recruiter on his own without my knowledge. Up for furlough from Ecuador, the former Baltimore County police officer and now missionary pilot had talked me into at least visiting and talking with a recruiter from each service branch.

It didn't take long for him to convince me that I probably did indeed need something drastic, like the military. I read a book by Robin Moore, *The Green Beret*, about a year before my discussion with my dad concerning my future. After some thought, I headed back to the army recruiter and asked the staff sergeant to tell me more about the Green Berets. My dad and mom had already departed back to Ecuador shortly after the holidays. The recruiter's sales pitch snagged me, hook, line, and sinker as I pictured myself training and helping indigenous people in tribes and villages around the world to fight Communism.

The Special Forces is just what I need! Before the ink was dry on the forms to sign my life away to Uncle Sam, I envisioned myself as one of the elite. To get there, I would have to become accustomed to jumping out of planes.

Both of my parents were shocked to discover what I had done. My mother was against me going into the military from the start. But despite my mother's resistance, the time came for me to leave, and I took the bus down to Miami and pledged to defend the Constitution against enemies, foreign and domestic. Next thing I knew, I was on a jet airliner flying to St. Louis in route to Fort Leonard Wood for basic training. Then, it was onward to Fort Benning, Georgia.

In just moments after getting settled, the planes revved into action and lurched forward with a jerk, one after the other. Then, with little time to think too deeply about what we were prepared to do, the three planes were airborne with their contents packed with soon-to-be paratroopers. There was no time to get comfortable. Action began almost immediately with every shouted command. The first one came abruptly.

"*Six minutes,*" the jumpmaster yelled while holding up five fingers on one hand and his thumb from the other!

"*Six minutes,*" we all echoed back with a shout.

Think quickly now; listen carefully!

Training mode set in, and I was on autopilot!

"*Outboard personnel, stand up!*" I could barely hear the screaming commands above the noise of the jet engines.

Had it been six minutes already?

Those of us sitting with our backs toward the exterior of the aircraft stood up clumsily, bumping into the soldiers on either side of us in the process.

"*Inboard personnel, stand up!*"

To complicate matters, now those facing the exterior of the plane stood up, knocking into us and causing some to lose their footing. I held out my hand trying to grab anything to keep me from falling down.

"*Hook up!*" the jumpmaster continued to yell.

After repeating this command, we all hooked our metal clasps attached to our yellow static lines to a cable running the length of the aircraft from front to back. Metallic clinking sounds could be heard above the droning of the jet engine.

"*Check static line!*"

After repeating the commands, we all complied, making sure that there was no visual damage, such as frays or tears with the line running down the back of the trooper in front of us. Then we turned around to repeat the process with the ones behind us.

"*Check equipment!*"

I looked at myself to make sure that all fastening devices were intact and that nothing had come loose. I did not want to be separated from my parachute once I exited the aircraft.

"*Sound off for equipment check!*" The jumpmaster's commands were in rapid progression.

The last soldier facing the jumpmaster was the closest one to the front of the aircraft as we faced the rear. He slapped the soldier in front of him and yelled, "*Okay!*"

The domino effect of slapping the rear of the soldier in front of him and yelling, Okay, continued down the line until I felt the hard slap on my cheek, immediately prompting me to do likewise to the trooper in front of me.

"*Okay!*" I yelled with vigor.

Then the process continued until the last slap reached the soldier standing directly in front of the jumpmaster standing at the door. He looked the jumpmaster square in the eyes and yelled at the top of his lungs, "*All okay, jumpmaster!*"

Everything was by the book so far. The butterflies inside me flapped faster and faster.

"*Two minutes!*" The jumpmaster continued to yell.

We did all that in four minutes?

The air was gushing in through the door as we stood looking around, sweating and trying not to look scared to our peers.

"*One minute!*"

The tension increased. My heart beat faster. I swallowed hard.

"*Thirty seconds!*"

No time to change my mind now!

"*Stand by!*" The jumpmaster was positioning himself to aid those exiting the aircraft, or to make sure that they *did* leave out the door.

"*Stand in the door!*"

Then the jumpmaster firmly grabbed the static line from the first jumper while the jumper walked toward the open door of the jet plane. The light over the door was red. He stood frozen, waiting for the signal. The sound of the wind gushing through the open side door along with the jet engines made it difficult to hear.

Wind gushed through the open door of the jet. The red light above the door turned green. "*Go!*"

The soldier in front of me began moving, and I found myself following like a robot, inching closer and closer to the open door. My mind was in the fast lane thinking of all the things I had trained to do in the past three weeks, all leading up to this very moment.

Then, in seconds, before I knew it, the soldier in front of me vanished. It happened so fast. I looked into the eyes of the jumpmaster and handed him my static line, not wanting anything bad to happen. Then I put my head down, my hands over my reserve and began walking forty-five degrees toward the open door of the jet aircraft.

"*Woosh!*" *I was a fastball that had just been thrown by Nolan Ryan!* I began my count, "One thousand, two thousand, threeeugh" as a tremendous jerk yanked me higher into the sky. I yelled like a spectator at a sporting event!

After quickly looking up to check my "can of peas"—the name the black hats used to jokingly refer to the canopy—I made sure that there were no tears or rips of any kind. Then I looked around for the other jumpers, making sure I was well clear of any flybys.

The song, "Sailing," by Christopher Cross, came to mind since it was heard over and over again on the jukebox during breaks. Another song was also popular during that time, but I didn't want to think about that one from Queen, "Another One Bites the Dust."

Then, the ground came rushing up toward me, and I had to turn my thoughts back to training mode and remember the techniques. The exhilaration of sailing through the air was way too short. I prepared myself for the PLF—point of landing fall—and executed a smooth and otherwise anticlimactic landing on the ground.

I got up and watched the dotted sky as other paratroopers sailed to the ground, all calmly attached to their wide-open chutes. I then began the process of rolling up my chute and packing it into the carry bag. *"Thank you, Lord, for being with me and seeing me through,"* I prayed.

We had five jumps in all. The fifth took place on the final day of Airborne School. This last jump was followed by a brief ceremony where the commandant pinned brand-new silver wings on our chests. I was now officially a US Army paratrooper. The sweat running down my cheeks didn't seem to be so bad at that moment, and I couldn't hold back a smile.

Chapter 3

Southern Pines, North Carolina
September 1980

I sprawled out on the damp turf, well hidden within the alluvial, humus, and understory of the woods. The strong smell of pine assailed my senses every time a breeze swirled through the air. Blending in with the foliage, I wore a solid OD (olive drab) color shirt and trousers. A patrol cap with two "snake eyes" that glowed in the dark fit snuggly on my head, and I had pulled it down to the bridge of my eyes. The whole idea was not to be seen, to blend in with the natural surroundings.

Earlier I had smeared stripes of green, brown, and black war paint across my face, and I felt ready from the tip of my head to the soles of my jungle boots. I lay flat on my belly and pushed the stock of an M-60 machine gun tight against my shoulder and supported the barrel on the metal tripod that unfolded from the weapon. Then I calmly rested my soft leather gloves on this instrument of death. Focused, alert, I was in the groove and ready to fulfill my role as the far right flank of our team.

Distractions lingered as the waiting seemed like forever. I checked the belt of ammunition that fed into the breach of the machine gun. Then I checked it again. After a while I lost count of the number of times that I glanced down at my weapon to confirm that the ammo feed was correct and the belt was free to feed without jamming. I fiddled with the safety switch making sure it was in the fire position. My team was counting on me to lay down a field of fire that would be overwhelming to the enemy. If I dropped the ball, our entire team and our mission could end in disaster.

The quiet was suddenly disturbed by the distant sound of deuce and half truck engines above the dusk calls of the wildlife. I looked down the line hoping that everyone was fully concealed. Checking my weapon for the last time I waited for the signal to open fire. The signal would be unmistakable; it was to be the sound of claymore mines ripping through the leaves.

Our team leader, Specialist Pippen, who had gone through Ranger school and was held in high regard by us young privates, had picked a great place for the ambush. The road wrapped around a sharp bend and then straightened out for a hundred-meter stretch. We were lined up on an elevated ridge that ran parallel to the road. The opposite side of the road was a steep slope that dropped into a thicket. Once we opened fire, the enemy would have a limited course of action and nearly nowhere to run or hide.

The first deuce rounded the corner followed by a couple of jeeps and two more Deuces. Patiently we waited. When all five vehicles hit the kill zone, we knew chaos would ensue.

Kaboom, kaboom, kaboom! The distinct sound of Claymore mines exploded. I carefully aimed at the rear deuce and began to unload a steady stream of devastating fire, cutting down anything that moved. The ridge exploded into action as our team unloaded, shredding the convoy. The barrage was over in seconds. Enemy vehicles staggered and swerved to a stop and bodies were strewn across the dirt road. My heart pounded. I was not sure how many rounds I had actually fired, but a quick glance at the pile of spent cartridges was all I needed to know. I had done my job.

As quickly as it had started, it was over. The firing stopped, and I shifted my field of fire and watched alertly for sudden movements as several of our team members jumped up from their hiding places and scrambled down the ridge to assess the carnage from their ambush. They quickly conducted a search of the bodies, taking precaution against the possibility of finding one of the wounded booby-trapped. The team completed the search in moments and retreated to its hiding place on the ridge.

We kept our game faces on despite the apparent victory. It was just as well. Before we could grin in satisfaction and slap each other on the back, our patrol leader barked out orders. "Let's go," he shouted, as he raced away from the ridge and into the woods, which was fast becoming very dark.

I jumped up along with the assistant gunner, and we took off following suit. Alongside us was the rest of the team, all racing up and down the waving slopes, through the trees, branches and creeks to our objective rallying point (ORP), where a small security team waited with our rucksacks. The only sounds that could be heard were clumping boots and snapping sticks as we sped through the fallen leaves and pine needles back to safety.

We continued running through the woods as the stars began to appear overhead; the correct exchange of passwords allowed us to pass the guards, where we grabbed our gear and moved swiftly to another designated rallying point. Once there, we would be able to sip water and catch a quick break.

As we rested against the trees an ominous figure approached. "Not bad. Not bad at all," he stated with a small grin. "But, we have another mission. Don't get too lazy. Be prepared to move out in ten."

I knew on the real battlefield we might not be given even this small break. It seemed relatively easy to ambush soldiers from the 82nd Airborne when everyone was firing blanks and throwing training grenades. But when the real lead began flying and the enemy was shooting back, any little mistakes on our part could get us killed.

We stifled our groans and hid our weariness, and we each did our last bit of preparation for the next mission. "Who's in charge for the next one?" I whispered to Breeden as he hefted his nearly one-hundred-pound rucksack over his back.

"Beats me. I've done mine, though."

"I haven't yet," I began. Just then, Specialist Pippen slid up to me.

"The TAC evaluators want to see ya now. You're up."

I looked over at Breeden, who smiled at me. "Do it, man."

"Thanks," I answered.

We were in the final week of our six-week Phase I training. One hundred and fifty-five soldiers arrived at Camp Mackall in three cattle trucks. We were down to fifty-five or so, divided up in three teams. Phase I of the "Green Beret" training had a nasty habit of separating the men from the boys, and I still even had doubts about myself. In fact, just two weeks prior to this patrol portion of training, I was on the verge of quitting.

"I've had it!" I remembered saying to myself. At least I thought I had. Oh how I missed the easy life, lying around on the couch in front of the tube watching *M*A*S*H* episodes on television or driving the white Pontiac Catalina convertible with red interior down to the clean beaches of Venice, Florida.

I was in pure misery. I lay shivering in the cold and soaked to the bone without a wink of sleep, unsuccessfully seeking comfort by burying myself deeper into the wet pine needles. Earlier, I'd gathered and stacked the driest pine needles I could find beneath the top-layered wet ones and made of them a bed of sorts underneath my leaky poncho.

It was only the second night of the Special Forces survival training, and I still had another night to go. The rain fell from the sky all day and night like an endless Victoria waterfall. The fact was I had not been dry in two days, since we'd had to hike through waist-deep water to get to our designated location. And, yes, we were quite alone and without food. *How bad do I want this green beret?*

I desperately needed a warm fire to dry myself out, but my few matches were hopelessly wet, and all that fancy talk about starting a fire by rubbing two sticks together only seemed to work on TV, never in reality. The nights were brutal. The cold rain did not let up. The temperature dropped, and the lack of activity caused my body temperature to plummet. Sleep was fleeting, and the shivers that racked my body woke me each time I rolled over, and a chilling breeze attacked a freshly exposed layer of skin.

While I battled the elements on the outside, there was another war being waged on the inside. One part of my mind was trying to convince me that I was a nobody and would never amount to much. *Go ahead and quit,* I would hear myself say. *Go back to your comfortable way of life and forget this misery.*

One night, while trying unsuccessfully to find sleep, those voices were quite audible, and they were not mine.

"Who's in here? Who's this? You alive?" I heard someone yell.

"Who the . . . ?" I began.

"Hey, is that you, Meehan?"

"Huh? Who's out there?" I slurred as I tried to regain control of my exhausted mind.

"Hey, a bunch of us guys have decided to bug out," he replied despondently. He continued, "Ya wanna join us?"

I hesitantly moved the wet pine needles off my chest and leaned on my elbow. I was really cold. And now, fully awake in the middle of a forsaken night, things could only get worse. If only I could have gotten a full night's sleep. But that dream had gone up in smoke as four to six of my fellow trainees stood over me shivering, ready to quit and wanting me to join them.

"Who's with you?"

The voice rattled off some names, and I noted that none of them included Mark Lupo, Dan Hall, Mike Yorgensen, or Hal Rodman. These guys had been with me since basic training at Leonard Wood, and we encouraged each other throughout our journey to this point.

Every inch of my miserable being and empty stomach wanted to say, *Okay, hold on a minute. I'm coming with you.*

But I didn't! No way was I going to let my buddies down, and I finally said, "Nah, go ahead without me. I'll hang for a while. Good luck."

"Aw right, man; maybe we'll catch you down the road."

I hope not. I thought to myself. "Sure thing; take care," is what I actually said.

Soon the chattering began again, and the rustling of the wet leaves being stomped on by jungle boots (I didn't really know how many) faded into the distance. I was alone again, except for my thoughts and the presence of God.

I prayed, *Lord, what was I thinking? Why didn't I go with them? Do I really need to prove myself?* I wasn't really sure, but maybe God had the answers. *Was it an induction into manhood? Would my family and friends be proud of me?*

For three days it had rained without relief—cold, steady, nagging, bone-chilling rain. Stomping around the hillside in my uniform with a poncho trying to accomplish the assigned tasks was just plain miserable. The poncho more or less kept my torso dry, but my arms from the elbows down and my legs from the thighs to my toes remained wet.

The survival portion was only a week after the land navigation part of the training. During that time, I found myself walking in circles on a hilltop while searching for my two-foot white marker during the night course. Based on my calculations and terrain features I felt sure that the sought-after metal pole was on this particular hilltop.

After several minutes of trudging along the soft, damp forest ground, layered with twigs, pine needles, and fallen autumn-colored leaves, I released the straps of my fifty-pound rucksack, and let it fall at my feet. Then, I plopped myself down against the trunk of a large tree, nearly pitch black in the dark of the night. The surrounding trees on this hilltop still whispered against the evening's cool wind. The dew began to settle beneath the night sky.

Despite the low, fifty-degree-and-dropping temperature, I wiped the sweat from my brow after tilting my patrol soft-cap slightly upward from my eyes. Sitting there was soothing and calm. I reached for my canteen and took a swig of iodine-laced water as droplets ran down my chin. I did not feel alone, but I was, physically anyway. The silhouetted stick figures were just that, tree branches and limbs protruding from the ground, some of which were swaying back and forth. It was a rare tranquil moment for me.

Earlier in the day, I found the appropriate landmarks within the allotted time that were necessary to successfully complete the Special Forces land navigation course. I needed to find four points during the daylight hours, at a distance stretching several kilometers over woodland terrain. Not long after arriving back to the base camp, the golden rays of sunlight that arrayed their light through the cerulean blue sky to the verdant hues in variegated shades on the Carolinian floor faded quickly to the graying dusk. The next task was to find two distinct landmarks at night, one of which led me to my current serenity.

The coal-colored sky provided a backdrop of light; light that sparkled like diamonds against clear endless space. The constellation struck me as pure, intangible, and idyllic. I felt like a part of the created cosmos, a small speck in the mass, twinkling, and infinite universe. The intake was calm and mysterious, something to take in depth and slowly; a moment to ponder.

I had a task at hand, however, and, based on my calculations, time was slipping away. I was confident about being at the right location, a lone hilltop surrounded by flatland, slopes, and draws. The trouble was that I circled this high point for too long without spotting the sharp, metallic, white-painted post that would give me the correct code number and the eight-digit grid coordinates to my next location. Without this information, I was a fish out of water and would not pass the land navigation course.

I quietly prayed, referring to the third chapter of Proverbs concerning trusting completely in God. The verses also said to acknowledge the creator in everything. This seemed like as good a time as any. After finishing with my prayer, I noticed something that I hadn't seen before. Among the curved and twisted protruding silhouetted branches and small trees, there in the midst was a small rigid limb without any bends, standing straight up toward the heavens. With my eyes fixated on this peculiar object, I slowly crawled over to find with much delight the metal post with the key data I was looking for.

Once I obtained all the information I needed, I hefted the rucksack over my back and adjusted the straps tightly. When I stood to look at the post, I could not see it because it blended into the black ground. It was only when I viewed my situation from an entirely different perspective (ground up) looking out into the starry sky, could I have seen the marker. I glanced one more time at the serene sky. Thank you, Lord! Then I scurried down the hill top toward my next destination. *"Mark the place where God has spoken"* *(Genesis 35:14 NLT).*

Toward dusk of the third day of survival, the remnants of the sun sparkled through the departing clouds, and the forest came to life. Out of nowhere, a truck engine roared, and with the sound getting closer, the vehicle finally appeared and then pulled up to my location. One of the instructors emerged with a live chicken in his hands.

"Just what the doctor ordered?" he half asked, half stated.

"Sure," I answered, trying to feel ecstatic about the prospect of becoming a manly man by killing a helpless chicken and then eating it.

I was able to finally get a fire started on the last day, and when it came time for me to meet the basic necessity of eating food, I audibly apologized to the fowl and proceeded to end its life quickly, as trained, and then ensured that nothing of this creature was wasted as I devoured the open-fire roasted chicken for my first meal in three days.

I slept fitfully that third night, and didn't wake again until the sun's rays pierced the sky and came to rest on my almost lifeless body in the early hours of dawn. Warmth conquered the chills, and for the first time in days, I actually experienced some degree of comfort.

Good morning, Lord! The air was still, crisp, and cool except for the arms of the sun. Not long after this moment of serenity, the peace and quiet was shattered by a throng of soldiers breaking through the woods. One of the instructors appeared leading an entourage of those who had their sites already inspected. It was my turn to receive the evaluation to determine whether or not I actually accomplished anything while surviving.

I answered a few of his questions and then after policing my area he told me to join them. After several stops to check other positions, we loaded up into a deuce and half cargo truck and without any fanfare headed back to Camp Mackall.

I had made it through that portion. I had survived. It was over. The journey into manhood faced and another challenge conquered. There would be little time for rest, nourishment, and reflection. I still had the patrols ahead of me to complete.

"Meehan!" The voice of the TAC officer snapped my reminiscing of the previous weeks of training. "You're up for the next mission!"

I was chosen as an assistant squad leader, and our mission was not unlike the previous missions. It went well. Then there were only two days left of the six-week grueling course. I was going to make it.

Finally, the last day, I found myself on familiar turf, stretched out on my stomach lying in the damp grass with our team awaiting one final mission to secure an airstrip. I glanced at my watch and held the button for a split second to view the green illumination. "0100."

"What time is it?" Private Nelson asked me, seeing that I was staring at my watch and playing with it to stay awake?

"Oh-dark-hundred."

"That figures."

The date showed 19 October 1980.

"Hey, whada ya know," I whispered to PV2 Nelson. "It's my birthday today!"

"Happy birthday," Nelson moaned. "How old?"

I had to think for a minute. "Twenty-two."

"You're an old man." Nelson chuckled. "We'll be able to celebrate after today."

"Let's hope," I added.

Six hours later, I discovered with tired elation that I was indeed one of fifty-two trainees who were still left after the six-week phase one course, and I would be able to move on with the Special Forces training into phase two. What relief! What quiet, tired, jubilance!

The voices inside the cattle-truck ride back to Fort Bragg were much fewer, but a lot noisier than when we had arrived six weeks before. The one roomy truck would haul us back to Fort Bragg and our new civilized barracks. After we were given our room assignments in a nice brick building, I felt like I had arrived!

A day or so later, we marched down to the supply room and received our green berets. I felt proud after receiving mine and became quite meticulous about wearing it properly. However, there was something unique about this particular beret. The velvety green cloth I donned in place of my old baseball cap had a thin white strip sewn on the front indicating to the world that we were still candy stripers—a white stripe sewn onto the front of the beret rather than a full patch—and had not yet arrived onto the big scene. We were yet to become bona-fide, fully qualified members of the elite Special Forces.

There would still be two more very tough phases ahead to finish before I could proudly wear the full flash patch on my beret. And for those of us who desired to be 18 Deltas, the code designator for Special Forces medics, the training would last for several more tough months.

CHAPTER 4

FORT BRAGG, NORTH CAROLINA
1980

I was arrogant even though I only had a candy stripe. The "full flash" would not come unless we completed the next two phases. Private Mark Lupo, along with three others that I had trained with since basic training at Fort Leonard Wood, also made it along with me through to the next phase. I wasn't surprised in the least about him making it; he was the distinguished honor graduate at basic training. A dark-haired, tan-looking man from Alabama with deep brown eyes; he was the epitome of a Special Forces soldier in my mind, and I secretly wished that my running skills and knowledge could come close to his.

Despite a southern drawl that would indicate he was an easy-going person, Mark was all business and had little time for nonsense; that is, until he was with us and away from training.

The others were Dan Hall, Mike Yorgensen, and Hal Rodman. Together we laughed, encouraged each other, and sweated through basic, AIT (advanced individual training) in San Antonio, Airborne School at Benning, and then, phase one at Fort Bragg, North Carolina.

Two months prior to our phase one completion, we disembarked from the bus at Fort Bragg on a humid Friday evening in August that took us from Fort Benning following Airborne School. We were met by two authentic Special Forces soldiers, whose green berets had the full flash sewn on. These were the first two Green Berets I had ever seen in person. One of them, the short, stocky, squared-jawed one, was wearing glasses and sported a mustache. The other, seemingly his sidekick, was tall and gangly with boyish eyes. Both wore their hair short from what I could see under their berets in the twilight, and neither of them were smiling nor acting as if they were glad to see the new set of recruits.

The short one, Staff Sergeant Weddle, spoke first. "All right, when I call your name, sound off!" He ordered.

I waited for the calling of my name. "Meehan!"

"Here, Sergeant!" I yelled back and then drifted back into my daydream state of mind, trying to take in the surroundings.

That is, until Weddle got to the name "Walker."

"Walker!" He repeated with irritation.

My memory jarred, I sheepishly and reluctantly answered for him. "Walker told me that he was driving up in his POV (privately owned vehicle)."

"What?" Staff Sergeant Weddle snapped looking right at me with glaring eyes. "Who told him he could do that?"

I was about to answer back, "Not me," when he continued. "Never mind, I'll deal with him Monday."

Weddle walked right up into the chest of the tallest guy in the group, PV2 Don Feakin, and said, "I'm leaving you in charge of these guys this weekend, and when I pick you up Monday morning, there better not have been anything that went wrong! You got that?"

Six feet, four inch, Don answered in a slow, deep, "John Wayne" drawl, "Yes, Sergeant!"

That weekend, however, everything that could go wrong did go wrong. First, one of the soldiers left his official orders on the bus. Orders were actually a piece of paper detailing one's next assignment, a document that each receiving unit would need in order to process the soldier into their system. These orders were now on the bus heading back to Fort Benning, Georgia, that night. The soldier talked Private Walker, who had arrived on Saturday morning in his POV, into driving him down to Georgia for a small fee so he could find them.

The following day, Sunday, after a successful mission retrieval of the orders, Walker had another soldier, Private Nelson, with him in his car when things went from crazy to insane. Private Walker, with Nelson as his passenger, was traveling along when another driver ran a stop sign and plowed into them, T-boning Walker's vehicle.

It could have been a lot worse, but Nelson still required several stitches to repair the gash in his head.

When Monday rolled around, Sergeant Silcose came to haul us to an old area of the base off of Bragg Boulevard. He didn't ask many questions. I supposed he was going to leave that to Staff Sergeant Weddle. We arrived in front of old-style barracks, which were separated from the rest of Fort Bragg. Two Vietnam era jeeps were parked out front and were just large enough to pile and squeeze in all twelve of us "wannabes." Welcome to the Special Forces!

Once the jeeps ground to a halt, Sergeant Silcose bellowed. "Everybody out and form up on the yellow line in front of the orderly room!" He pointed in the direction of a large painted yellow line that ran along the edge of a long blacktop driveway leading past several wooden two-story shacks located on both sides of the road. The buildings were typical housing units from the seventies, remnants from the Vietnam period painted white with dark green trim. Screen-covered doors were located at each end and in the middle. Quickly, we formed up on the line while Staff Sergeant Weddle simultaneously burst through the side doors of the barracks. His sudden appearance, followed by a loud bang as the door slammed shut behind him, caused the entire line to jump in unison.

He began methodically. "I heard that somebody left their orders on the bus," Staff Sergeant Weddle stated with an air of, you're mine now satisfaction as he descended the steps slowly.

"That would be me, Sergeant," a voice squeaked out from the end of the line.

Weddle pivoted on a dime and stomped toward the voice, "Who, said that?" He yelled, sounding much like a drill sergeant.

"I did," Private Artillo hesitantly volunteered.

"Well?" Weddle challenged, "What are you going to do now, hero?"

"I have them, Sergeant," Artillo said, with an air of uncertain victory.

"You, you do, how did you get them?" Weddle asked, stuttering with surprise defeat in his voice. He seemed perturbed that he'd lost the opportunity to make an example of such foolish irresponsibility, but like a dog with a bone, was unwilling to totally let go.

"Private Walker drov—" he was unable to finish his sentence when Weddle interrupted as a thought suddenly came to his mind.

"Walker? Where is he? Where are you, Private?" Weddle's voice was rising steadily.

Walker, who was standing right next to me, muttered a barely audible curse, "Here, Sergeant!"

Weddle picked up the pace with quick little steps until he came face-to-face with Walker. "So, you're Walker, the one who thinks he can do whatever he wants whenever he wants," Weddle began. I could see out of the corner of my eyes that Walker was flinching and blinking his eyes with every word that proceeded out of Weddle's mouth, which was laced with words that would curl one's hair or burn sensitive ears. I was trying hard to stifle a burst of laughter.

It was obviously clear that Weddle had found a new focus for his irritability since his initial plan of attack failed, and, like a shark that senses blood in the water, the sergeant moved in for the kill. Speaking a little louder and interlacing his growing tirade with curses, he lifted his right hand and began waving his index finger back and forth in front of Walker's nose. Suddenly, with mouth wide open and finger still raised, he froze with wide-eyed horror.

Inching his way one step to his right, he slowly lifted the baseball cap off of Private Nelson's head, revealing an oversize, bloodstained white bandage. Holding Nelson's hat in his hand, and with glaring eyes that could set a forest afire, Weddle managed to finally spit out, "What in the name of God happened to you?"

Nelson could hardly speak, but was able to meekly eek out the words, "I was in a car wreck, Sergeant."

"A car wreck?" Weddle screamed with curses. "Whose car were you in?"

"Walk . . ." Nelson began, but it was too late, and hearing Walker whisper another curse, I braced myself for another tirade and wondered how I was going to make it through without erupting into laughter.

Weddle was already running back to the front of Walker, unleashing a tirade of mixed bile and spit that radiated a spray in my direction. I was sure Staff Sergeant Weddle could care less. I wasn't about to complain.

For the second time in a span of minutes, Weddle stopped in midstream with his finger raised and then nearly ran down the line to PV2 Don Feakin, the big man he had left in charge over the weekend. I had no doubt that a Green Beret NCO was secretly having an enjoyable time at our expense.

"I thought that I told you not to let anything happen to these soldiers this weekend," Weddle said, looking up at Feakin with fire in his eyes.

"Yes, Sergeant, you did," was all Feakin was able to say in his John Wayne drawl.

The look on Weddle's face showed no signs of fun and games, and I knew that the only intelligent way to survive was to keep my eyes forward and my mouth shut. It was extremely difficult to hold in an outburst of pent-up laughter, but hold it in I did. I had to, just as everyone else had to. These were the kind of moments I would laugh about much later with others who had experienced the same. But not now, not when we were being properly introduced to the Green Berets.

After we survived the "Prephase" training with Staff Sergeant Weddle, about 155 of us loaded onto cattle cars—silver metallic trucks that had benches along the outer skin of the vehicle and more benches backed against each other in the middle. There was also an upper platform, which could cram more soldiers in as long as they were knee-to-knee. The energy level was high. Every young recruit was sure he would save the world and defeat communism single-handedly. But the hard realities of phase one and the refined tearing down and building up process would soon begin winnowing the wheat from the chaff.

Boot camp at Fort Leonard Wood was a walk in the park compared to Special Forces training. Phase one of Special Forces training was much more challenging, both physically and mentally. The instructors were continuously messing with our minds and bodies. They knew the truth. Physical hardship needed to be overcome with a force of will and not just physical strength. A lot of mental fortitude was involved. The cold, harsh realities of being behind enemy lines doing special ops could break a man and leave not only the entire unit vulnerable, but a whole community.

CHAPTER 5

The "Pit" and the Phone Booth
Fort Sam Houston, Texas
1981

Although I was not a full-fledged Green Beret, the past accomplishments still went to my head. Arrogance on my part led me to partake in activities that did not always pass the common-sense test. I began frequenting a variety of nightclubs along Bragg Boulevard, Hay Street, and other such establishments that attracted young GIs who were party-minded.

During the long Thanksgiving weekend in 1980, Hal Rodman and I hopped a Greyhound bus and headed down to Venice, Florida, to visit my grandparents. The plan was to drive back in my 1964 Chevy Bel Air that had been kept for me throughout my previous seven months of training. I couldn't wait for the additional freedom a car would allow me to have back at Bragg while we waited for our phase two to begin.

Saturday night after Thanksgiving, Rodman and I went to a club called, Lido's, located in Sarasota. It was just up the highway, not far from where I had first joined the army. The night turned out to be uneventful except for the dancing and the stupor that I had allowed myself to get in that prompted Rodman to take charge of the return drive back to the mobile home in Venice. Fortunately, it was late, and my grandparents were already in bed. I had no trouble drifting into a deep sleep on the hide-a-bed sofa, although I couldn't get the song "Rock and Roll Fantasy," by Bad Company, out of my head.

Getting up early the next morning, Rodman and I, along with my grandparents, sat around the breakfast table just prior to our departure north. I was very close to both of them. Looking over at my grandparents, I somehow felt a gap, some sort of distance between them and me. It was a genuine lack of connection, a chasm.

My grandparents were very godly people whom I respected deeply and had grown up under their influence. They were saved at a Billy Graham crusade in Baltimore when my father was a young teen. It was this defining moment at the breakfast table that caused me to realize just how far I had allowed myself to slip into a worldly dependence.

That morning was my wake-up call, like somebody had just slapped me in the face. The reality of my soul's condition penetrated deeply. As Hal and I headed back to Bragg, the mesmerizing clicking of the tires skipping over the joints in the highway's concrete surface was hypnotic. When Hal fell asleep, I was left alone with my thoughts.

Here I was, a missionary's kid, the grandchild of godly grandparents, someone who knew right from wrong—someone who should have known better facing the harsh reality that I had been turning my back on God, and this was definitely not a good time to do it.

I searched for the living word in my heart. I felt as though God was revealing the words from Jeremiah 6:16, which said, "Stand in the crossroads and look; ask for the ancient paths, ask where the good way is, and walk in it, and you will find rest for your souls." *I needed that rest for my soul.* Then, when I asked God to forgive me, I remembered another verse from Psalm 40:2. "He lifted me out of a slimy pit, out of the mud and mire and set my feet on a solid rock and gave me a firm place to stand."

Both of those references from the Bible added together were pivotal to what I considered to be a real spiritual transformation. I was elated when we arrived back at Fort Bragg, and I felt like a different person than the one who went south for the weekend. My friends who had helped me through the tough times seemed a little confused by my spiritual conflict. I was relieved when our activities focused more on things like tackle football or halfway decent movies. I told them that I was finished with the club scene, though.

Less than a month later, all of us slotted for phase two at Fort Sam Houston in San Antonio, Texas, were given block leave for the Christmas holidays. I could sense a renewed desire to get closer to God through reading the Bible and prayer. I was going to spend my holidays back in Venice, Florida, with my grandparents, and this time be ready for a connection and a peace of mind.

Christmas went by quickly, and after driving across the panhandle of Florida, Alabama, Mississippi, Louisiana, and half of Texas, I pulled into the front gate at Fort Sam Houston. The skyline of San Antonio hadn't changed any in the six months since I had been there last. After receiving directions to where the Special Forces barracks were located, I pulled into the parking lot of two very old, white, two-story wooden barracks. Immediately coming out to greet me and welcoming me to the new living area were Mark, Mike, Hal, and Dan.

Mixed emotions ruled the moment. In the background, other Special Forces (SF) soldiers held a bottle of beer while surrounded by a variety of young ladies, often referred to as groupies. I was just like any other twenty-one-year-old, and the sight troubled me. *This is not what I need for the next thirteen weeks.* Though genuinely happy to see my closest buddies for the past nine months, I saw myself heading toward a spiritual challenge.

The Sunday evening before classes started early the following morning, I spotted an old-fashioned phone booth near the barracks, the kind Superman used. I went there with the appropriate number of coins and dialed my grandparents, assuring them that I arrived safely.

When I finished talking with them, I hung up the phone and started to walk away. After a few steps, I turned around, looked at the booth, hesitated, and then went back into the phone booth. Staring at the phone for a couple of seconds, I then picked it up. This time without dialing, I put the receiver to my ear, and spoke audibly into the mouthpiece.

"Lord, you better than anyone else understand my predicament, and how I feel about it. I don't want to fail you in any way. Please give me guidance as to what I should do here, and show me the way to make it through. Thank you."

I placed the phone back on the receiver, breathed a sigh of relief that nobody was around, and headed back to the barracks. I felt a sense of relief as I lay in my rack, drifting off to sleep. Everything would be all right.

Early Monday morning, the class of sixty aspiring SF soldiers filed into a non-air-conditioned World War II style wooden building, much like the ones where we were residing with our bunks side-by-side. The second floor was set up with classroom desks and chairs. Taking our seats, we waited for the staff of instructors to introduce themselves, and then the officer in charge (OIC), a doctor, Captain Kulingowski, MD, began a speech.

Somewhere in the middle of his speech, he made a startling announcement. "We have a unique situation here. Our course is designed for only sixty people, and the Alabama National Guard got their dates mixed up and sent four of their soldiers to this class." Captain K, as everybody would eventually call him, continued, "We cannot send these four soldiers back to their units because of state funding, so we have the difficult task of asking for four volunteers from the regular army to return to Fort Bragg until the next class."

He added. "If anyone of you wish to volunteer, come and talk with us during the break, and we will arrange your trip back. There will be no penalties, and you will be assured a slot in the next class. In fact, you should get plenty of time off while you wait."

I felt that this was my opportunity to seize. When we took a break shortly after Captain K's speech, I quickly sought one of the staff to express my desire to be one of the volunteers. I was sent to talk with Captain K himself and members of his staff about going back. Arrangements were made for me to return to Fort Bragg the following day.

"What were you thinking, man?" Mike asked. His question was followed by more of the same by Hal and Dan.

"I don't know, just a spur-of-the-moment decision I felt needed to be done," I answered. Only I knew that this was not entirely true.

"Well, good luck. We'll miss ya," Mike said.

"You'll catch up with us," Hal added.

"Good-bye, guys. I'll see you somewhere down the road."

I loaded up my '64 Chevy Bel Air and turned north to Dallas initially. I wanted to first see some of my MK friends from

Colombia before heading east to Carolina. All of the ones I came into contact with were encouraging me onward.

Although Captain K said there would be no penalties, I wasn't too certain how I would be received back at Bragg. I could be an outcast, for all I knew. *Would they be on me for lack of motivation? Would they consider me a quitter?* I wondered.

My fears turned out to be unfounded, as I was well received and given many tasks that needed to be completed around the Bragg area. I even joined a tae kwon do class for a few weeks.

Later, with too much time on my hands, I became restless and decided to request some leave time. My request was granted, and the only place I could think of escaping to at that moment was the Amazon jungles of Ecuador, where my missionary parents were on assignment for four years. It would be a refreshing change to get away and spend some time with the folks and our dog, Smokey. I looked forward to a three-week period of escape from the world.

CHAPTER 6

AMAZON EMERALDS
MARCH 1981

I was in another world, far removed from the intense training of Fort Bragg and Camp Mackall, North Carolina. I stared out the window of the Helio Courier, a light short takeoff and landing (STOL) utility aircraft. The all-aluminum airframe features a welded 15G steel-tube center-section fuselage, with shoulder harnesses to protect the occupants in an emergency. This aircraft was designed to maintain control at speeds as low as twenty-seven miles per hour.

The view below was inundated with long brown rivers slithering like snakes through the thick green jungle canopy that resembled an enormous broccoli patch. The pilot, Danny Rose, was my dad's friend and colleague, and, like my dad, he lacked hair on most all of his scalp. When out of the plane, he stood about five feet ten, and though not considered to be overweight, he was stout.

Our destination was a tiny enclave of sporadic houses making up a missionary base known as Limoncocha. The dozen or so homes at the edge of a lemon-shaped lake were deep in the Amazon jungle of Ecuador. It surrounded a grassy runway, long enough for a McDonald Douglas DC-3 to easily land and take off.

Many thoughts went through my mind as I looked out across the thick, vegetated, and mostly uninhabited land. Those, however, were interrupted by our descent onto the base airstrip, plenty long enough for the single-engine craft.

The plane taxied to a stop in front of the open-bay hangar that stood next to a wooden shack that served as the passenger terminal. Once the engine stopped, Danny gave me the thumbs-up, and I unbuckled my seatbelt and shoulder harness, opened the door, and stepped out into the thick air. The humidity was worse than I remembered, far worse than it was at Fort Benning, Georgia, during airborne school, when the temperature stood at a hundred degrees for nearly two straight weeks. Sweat poured down my cheeks before I could exert any motion. My designer shades slid down my nose.

My father came out to greet me from the hangar. He was the primary factor in my decision in joining the army fifteen months earlier. I had not seen him since then, when together we talked to the recruiters from all branches of service. He and my mother were in Venice, Florida, for the holidays and to celebrate my grandparent's fiftieth wedding anniversary. They traveled back to Ecuador about a day before I went back to the army recruiter and asked about joining the Special Forces.

My mother arrived to the hangar on her Honda 100 with our dog, Smokey, tagging along behind. Even he was excited to see me, expressed by his knack for bowling people to the ground. I held my ground, however, prepared for his manner of greeting. I traveled lightly, so I grabbed my bag and took over the bike and headed home. I was in a hurry to make a change of clothes.

After braking to a stop at the front of the house, I bounded up the steps into the open, screened, wooden frame built about three feet off the ground. With the sweltering heat attacking me, I wasted little time shedding my traveling threads and donning a pair of cutoff jeans and sleeveless T-shirt. With no air conditioning available, that would have to do.

While in the back bedroom changing, I heard my mother talking to someone from the kitchen. "Yeah, he's here," I heard her yell.

I was finished changing so I headed to the front area of the house to see who was behind the other female voice I was hearing. When I emerged from the back bedroom, I saw this pretty young lady. There she stood in the doorway, looking at me with those mesmeric eyes. She was indeed *A green-eyed lady, lovely lady-Sugarloaf!*

"Hi!" She greeted me with a radiant smile.

"Hello," I answered back, trying to hide my gawking toward such a good-looking woman.

"How was your trip?"

"It wasn't too bad; a bit lengthy." *She certainly is good-looking*, I thought.

"You remember Trena, don't you?" my mother asked.

I remembered meeting her briefly once before at a restaurant, *The Oyster Bar* in St. Petersburg, Florida. That was when several people from Ecuador were stateside during the holidays, including the time my parents were in Florida. I also remembered that we probably had not spoken more than a dozen words to each other the whole night. Although I would steal a glance in her direction whenever I thought her attention was somewhere else and I could get away with it, I don't believe she was the least bit interested in me.

Why would she have been? I had just dropped out of my first attempt at college, and my hair was shoulder length. Trena, on the other hand, already had her master's degree.

"Yes, at that restaurant in Florida, I believe."

"Yep, I remember," she said. "Well, good seeing you again. I just got off work and need to go change, but I'll be back."

"Okay." That's all I could think to say at the moment.

Trena had just finished teaching the missionary kids at the base school. "She comes over now and then, so we'll probably see her shortly," my mother mentioned.

I was glad to hear that. Sure enough, maybe thirty minutes later, she was back. This time, she was wearing a T-shirt and a pair of shorts that revealed her nicely bronzed legs. I was impressed, to say the least. Trena sat down and began what seemed to be a routine chat with my mother. It may have been my imagination, but she seemed more interested in looking at me this time around. My appearance had certainly changed. I just completed army basic training, airborne school, and phase one of the Special Forces (SF) training. My hair was much shorter, and my frame was more muscular.

I chimed in on the conversation occasionally, mainly trying not to let it appear too obvious that I was watching her with admiration. Trena was tall and slim, at least five feet, eight inches, and her dark brown hair was shoulder length. But it was the glow of her effervescent smile and the sparkling green emerald eyes that captured my undivided attention. I was in trouble. Although I was definitely attracted to her, I needed to hide those feelings, at least for the time being. I certainly didn't want to say or do anything that might chase her away.

Trena definitely was not one of the SF camp groupies that hung around at the barracks, nor was she one of the girls that frequented the clubs. In fact, she was considered by many to be an overachiever, blowing first through high school in three years followed by a mere three more to complete her bachelor of arts. Her master's degree was completed shortly after that, while she was teaching in Clearwater at the age of twenty-two!

The granddaughter of a Nansemond Indian chief of the Powhatan Empire, Trena attacked everything with grit and determination. She was not only driven but dedicated. How else could one explain the presence of a young, beautiful woman doing mission work in the middle of the Amazon jungle?

Trena's sharp cheekbones curved smoothly into a lovely face framed by dark brown hair. Those exquisite, oval, emerald green eyes seemed to sparkle with intelligence, delight, and just a touch of mischief. I was definitely enamored by her striking features.

If I ever stood a chance with this appealing young lady I would need to develop a strategic plan to earn her affections. I needed a plan that would include developing a deep friendship, if that was possible in three weeks, and one that would avoid any chest-pounding self-bravado and machismo.

Since our conversations began with simple small talk surrounding common interests, my strategy was starting off in the right direction. I intended on not telling her anything about my training unless she asked. I figured that my mother already took care of all that anyway. Our mutual friendship continued along this path for ten days, but I was okay with it because I simply enjoyed being around her.

It was during this time that Trena left for a three-day visit to one of the mission's remote tribes, the Sequoya village of San Pablo. She would be visiting an American couple working with translation. About the same time, my dad asked me if I wanted to go on an excursion to a different tribe. The purpose for our trip was to inspect a recently hacked out (with machete) airstrip.

My dad would determine if the strip was suitable for landing and subsequent frequent airlifts into and out of that village.

The Waoranis tribal people lived in the Quiwado village. They were once referred to as the Aucas because of their reputation of being head-hunters. In fact, these were the natives who martyred five American missionaries in the late '50s. In 1965, a Wycliffe missionary came home on furlough in Baltimore and spoke to the church congregation about missions. My dad, a Baltimore County police officer at the time became interested. The missionary, George Gardner, gave my dad a book called *Jungle Pilot,* a story about Nate Saint, one of five murdered missionaries in Ecuador during the late '50s.

Our trip would involve an overnight in a nearby village and then an early morning start toward the Quiwado village. It was during this first night away from Trena when I realized I could not get her image out of my mind. I did not even want to. As I lay on my mat on the dirt floor inside a mud hut, waiting to find some sleep, I attempted to sort through my feelings about her. What was it about this girl? *She's really got me now.* Was I in love? It had been a long time since I'd had a relationship with a girl that was meaningful.

The next morning, my dad and I, along with two native guides, began our hike through the jungle on our way to the Quiwado village. Having recently completed phase one of SF training, I hiked with ease, staying with the lead guide, step-by-step. After all, there was no hundred-pound ruck on my back this time; no M-16 or M60 to haul around either. I wore hiking shoes, a long-sleeved T-shirt, and blue jeans and was armed with a small hunting rifle.

I felt like I was flying through the jungle, but the only living creatures that were flying were quite beautiful to behold. Both varieties of the large Macaw parrots flew in small flocks above us on more than one occasion. I was enthralled by the blue and gold as well as the bright red birds.

I was able to enjoy the surroundings more than my dad, since the lead guide and I had to stop frequently to wait for him and the rear guide helping him. The ground was wet and slippery with mud in some spots, dry in others. Long vines drooped from the tall trees. Water dripped from the leaves after a short cloud burst of rain. The hike through the Amazon jungle, which included a large river crossing on a balsa wood raft that the guides hacked out in thirty minutes, took four hours. By then, I was used to the sounds of the insects' constant chirping and buzzing.

As we approached the village, we were greeted by the native women, who brought us a bowl of *chicha*. My dad warned about this drink ahead of time, but he also told me to just drink it and don't think about it. *Chicha* consisted of chewed bananas that were spit back into a community boiling pot over an open fire that helped ferment the warm brew. I took a gulp. I thought about something else.

The villagers bathed in the nearby river, the men and then the women, separated. The water was cool and refreshing. Our first night at the village consisted of bathing, communications, eating dinner, and sleeping on the hard floor made of sticks. With no electricity, this all began with the sinking of the sun below the jungle canopy. It was my second night away from Trena, and I still couldn't get her out of my head. I did not sleep well.

We had breakfast the next morning prepared by the villagers, and then we began the task of inspecting the airstrip from one end to the other and everything in between. Dad made the call to Danny Rose and told him it looked good, and we would wait for him to pick us up.

While waiting, I occupied myself by taking photos of the local villagers, and made friends with many of the children. The day wore on until we all heard the distant buzz of the Helio propeller ripping through the sky with its distinct sound. Many of the villagers ran onto the airstrip to watch the plane land but were quickly chased away by the chief and my dad and redirected to a vantage point off of the strip.

I snapped a picture as the plane touched down, and as it sped past us, the villagers rushed out onto the strip after the plane as a group of college students would rush the basketball court after a last-second victory. The aircraft taxied to a stop, and Danny was quickly surrounded by a lot of village people. He was the first pilot to ever land on Quiwado strip. Danny got out of the plane and started shaking hands with everyone as if he was a president. Then he and my dad broke away and began walking the airstrip together discussing all of the technical intricacies.

After two days away from Limoncocha and a memorable hike through the jungle topped off with *chicha*, Danny, my dad, and I boarded the plane and safely took off, leaving the waving villagers behind. My thought turned to other matters.

Realizing that my time in Ecuador would only last another ten days, I had to think of ways to expedite my strategic plan of winning Trena over. I had no idea how she felt about me, but it was time to find out.

I made it a point to visit her after dinner that first evening back. Trying to keep my cool and playing hard to get, I made the excuse that I wanted to read the up-to-date *Newsweek* magazines she had lying around the table in her little dwelling. With a nice comfortable hammock strung up next to the stack, I thought of this as a good place to start. I wanted to stay abreast of the situation in El Salvador, especially since I could very well end up there within a year. I also wanted to read the sad story about one of my friends, Chet Bitterman, who had been kidnapped and then had been executed by the M-19, the same guerilla faction that had nearly blown me up four years earlier.

Grabbing the *Newsweek* from Trena's table, I made my way to the local handmade hammock. I then settled in and buried my face in the magazine, flipping pages, and trying to carry on a conversation as she was completing her dishwashing. *Okay, Lord, if she's the one, something has to happen.* Then I pondered a way to make a move without making a fool of myself. Various scenarios began to run through my mind.

Bam! Suddenly, the impact of a rubber ball against the magazine in my hand slapped like a gunshot. Stunned at first, I reacted with lightning quick reflexes, spinning to take cover. Then I realized that not only had Trena thrown a ball at me, but she was moving quickly to retrieve it. Nothing doing, I thought. I rolled out of the hammock quickly, and scrambled in the direction the ball had rolled. Prevention of another attack was on my mind as both of us reached for the ball instantaneously.

"Ah-hah!" I grunted while grabbing the ball.

"Not fast enough, slow poke!" Trena laughed back as she viciously began prying it out of my tight grip. Before I knew the full gist of what was happening, I realized that we were involved in a semiwrestling match. Within moments our arms were twisted together trying to get the ball out of the other's hand.

Trena struggled to turn, trying to pull away, but she was no match for me. As she spun, with one final thrust, I reached out, caught her hand, and drew it back toward me, and we suddenly found ourselves face-to-face within inches from each other. I caught my best glimpse yet of her gorgeous green eyes. They were only about three inches away. We both momentarily froze.

I couldn't help but stare deeply into her entrancing eyes, which had me so mesmerized. I did not want to move an inch. Then, slowly, without any apparent decision or plan, we simultaneously inched closer toward each other until our lips softly touched and stayed together for about four seconds. We released our tight grip on each other's hands but kept them together as we moved toward each other again, this time for a longer-lasting kiss. I must admit that I did feel a riveting surge sweep over my whole body. Why not? I was in the midst of enjoying a lasting kiss with the knockout girl that had captivated me, both with her beauty and with her friendship. I wanted our first kiss to be one to remember a lifetime!

"I've been waiting for a girl like you
To come into my life"—Foreigner

The Meehans in the jungles of southern Mexico in front
of our homemade house (1972)

Before the army—hitchhiking in South America (1979); after the
army—waiting for an airborne operation at Fort Sam Houston, Texas (1981)

CHAPTER 7

MARRIAGE
SALEM, VIRGINIA
OCTOBER 1981

The jet from Ecuador touched down in Miami, but I was still flying at high altitude. *Were those three weeks in the jungle a mere dream?* Thankfully, it was real, and I had met my match! Saying good-bye to Trena was a lot more difficult than I had imagined it would be. I had a feeling that this new desire for her could possibly come in conflict with my previous desire to become a Green Beret.

Back at Fort Bragg, I was rooming with new SF trainees who would be going through the next phase with me back in Texas. Mark Voydik, a wrestling champion from Schkulhaven, Pennsylvania, had missed the previous training phase while recovering from a touch football injury. Mark and I hit it off great, and he ended up traveling back west with me in my Bel Air.

Trena and I kept in touch through the (what is now known as snail) mail. Letters took a full two weeks to travel from Ecuador to Texas. One of the letters contained the news that Trena's two-year term would be coming to an end and that she would be home in Roanoke, Virginia, about the same time that my thirteen-week course would end.

I was counting the days! My next assignment would take me to Fort McClelland, Alabama, for six weeks of on-the-job training at the Noble Army Hospital. When the course ended, I sold my camera, purchased a plane ticket with the money, and flew to Roanoke to get reacquainted with Trena and solidify our relationship. Another colleague, PFC Rooney, drove my Bel Air to Fort McClelland.

The week at her parents' home was, in a sense, a recon trip, and it was my task to analyze the data. The week in Virginia was a success! I had confirmed my speculation. On the trip to Alabama, I began my debriefing. Final analysis: I, or rather, we, were in love.

There wasn't a night that I failed to call Trena from the hospital pay phone. Expressing my feelings over the phone had its shortcomings. It just wasn't working well. There was something about standing at a pay phone, feeding quarters into the machine and being interrupted and reminded that you had only thirty seconds left and needed to feed more money into the machine that wasn't conducive to a romantic conversation.

One weekend in July, we made plans to meet at my parents' stateside house outside of Johnson City, Tennessee. My grandparents were staying there for the summer, escaping the Floridian heat while my parents were still in Ecuador. We would have the weekend together, and I was really looking forward to it.

The sun was setting over the rolling hills of Tennessee as we sat together in the den, holding each other and not wanting to let go. Every time I looked into her eyes, my heart melted, and I was captivated once again.

Finally, with her subtle prompting, because I was either being naïve or dense, I asked her to marry me. To my sheer delight, she said, "Yes, of course I will!"

I didn't know what to do next other than to say, "Really? Cool! All right!" Inside, I was jubilant! We immediately gave the news to my grandparents, who seemed to be quite pleased. Then we made the numerous phone calls, one of which was *the* phone call to her dad when I asked permission for Trena's hand in marriage. He answered, "Yeah, okay, I guess it's all right."

The next three months were a blur as we prepared for the wedding. Tim Goring, another MK from Colombia, and Steven Birge, my college roommate at my failed attempt at Taylor University, were asked to be in my wedding. My brother, Russ, could not make it. My dad would be my best man, a thought that came by way of Eddie Gilchrist.

Seven months after our first kiss we were married in a small church in Salem, Virginia, nestled within the colorful autumn leaves, which was typical of the Shenandoah Valley. A cool, brisk wind was blowing that night, the night never to forget.

She was absolutely stunning when she came down the aisle in her wedding dress, escorted by her father. The ceremony was a daze, but I distinctly remember staring into Trena's beautiful green eyes as they were transfixed on mine. She had the look of love and admiration, and as we stood hand-in-hand on the altar, I felt with heartfelt sincerity that I would love her until the day I died. Thirty-two years later, I still feel the same way.

After a great honeymoon week at my grandparents' mobile home (they were still in Tennessee) we traveled back to Fayetteville, North Carolina, and settled into a small two-bedroom green trailer. It was located at the runway edge of Pope Air Force Base in Spring Lake, North Carolina.

As we opened our wedding gifts together, we lovingly cuddled and laughed together like the newlywed couple that we were and began our new lives together. Two months after marriage, Trena was carrying our first child.

It was three months after our wedding that I began the next phase of SF training. However, after much thought and prayer (certainly not a spur-of-the-moment decision), I made a choice. Two weeks into our last advance medical training, an eight-week medical lab conducted back at Fort Bragg, I approached the class sergeant and told him that I needed to talk with him when he had time. He was ready to listen immediately and asked me what I needed to talk about.

I let the words that had been on my mind for a while finally escape my lips.

"I want to voluntarily terminate my Special Forces training." *There, I said it,* I thought to myself.

He just looked at me dumbfounded. "Are you sure you want to do this?"

"Yes," I said meekly. I probably should have answered, "No, not really, but can I do this lab later?"

"If you're sure about this, I'll take you to one of the training sergeants."

"All right, I'm ready to talk with him now." I wasn't feeling so confident.

The next three-day process of talking to several sergeants and officers along the chain of command was torturous. One colonel was actually beside himself with rage that I would dare quit voluntarily from the Green Beret training after being so far along. It quickly struck me that I probably would have made it if I had stayed with the program.

Too late now. No, I'm making the right decision. I chose to get married and begin a family because I desired that more than obtaining a Green Beret.

I married Trena knowing full well what I was doing, and two months later she was carrying our first child. My enthusiasm for obtaining the coveted Green Beret had diminished to where it fell way down on my priority list. I knew that if I was going to complete the course successfully and then become an elite soldier, I would have to give it my all. I wasn't sure that I could do that anymore. My mind was preoccupied with other things, like my wife and future child.

Trena had told me all along that it was my decision to make and that she would accept and support whatever I chose. She was already sick every day during her first month, and the fact that I came home at night smelling like a goat didn't help matters any. Now was the time, and I had made my decision. I was ready to move on and take care of my family instead of pursuing a patriotic zeal to become one of America's elite.

The manner in which I presented my decision to the cadre didn't make too many of them very fond of me. When I received my new orders sending me to a different unit, I discovered that I had been sent to a nonairborne unit and that my jump status was taken away. I heard that once this was done, it was nearly impossible to gain it back again.

Matters became much worse when I reported to my unit, a field artillery leg-nonairborne unit, and found that the regular, conventional army was as different from the Special Forces as night was from day.

I immediately let my superiors know that being sent here was a mistake and that I would be working toward getting my jump status back. This would be preceded by a move down the street to the Eighty-Second Airborne Division.

Early on my second morning, I was approached by a second lieutenant from the medical section. He offered to assign me to special duty status working regular hours without any formations or field duty at the troop medical clinic for six months. The only condition was that I had to stay with the 1/39th Field Artillery to obtain this special duty. I asked him when he needed to know the answer. He wanted it by the next day because only he and the commander knew about this.

I talked it over with Trena, who was excited about the idea of me being home at regular times without going out to the field for a period of time. I was also, for that matter, especially since I had only one year left on my current enlistment.

I went back to the second lieutenant the next day and accepted his offer. Then, the day after, I reported to my new duty at the clinic, where I would become one of the senior screeners of patients during sick call at Troop Medical Clinic 15.

The value I gained during this period by helping others with their physical problems was only surpassed by the fact that I was home with Trena, who remained sick throughout her pregnancy. I was home when she nearly lost the baby at five months because it was discovered that she had an incompetent cervix—a condition in which she would not be able to contain the baby without surgery.

Fortunately, since the Fort Bragg hospital maternity section was so full, Trena was allowed to choose a doctor off post, and it was his quick discovery that placed Trena immediately into surgery in order to perform a McDonald circlege and sew the baby in her womb. I was given a three-month extension to work in the clinic, thanks to the support of the medical staff assigned there.

Finally, I was home and able to witness the delivery of our first child, Aaron Scott, on the thirteenth of September 1982. Trena and I considered Aaron our miracle baby due to all the circumstances leading to his birth. Circumstances? I should know better by now. God's orchestration is the more appropriate term. He had a plan for us, and we were moving forward.

When I left the Special Forces command, I was reassigned to the Eighteenth Field Artillery Brigade and began practicing my medical skills at Troop Medical Clinic 15 (TMC 15). With the mentorship of very knowledgeable medical professionals like Sergeant Welch, Chief Warrant Office 4 Shank and Chief Warrant Officer 2 Champion, I felt as if I was on course for a medical career. I earned an expert field medical badge (EFMB) and reenlisted for another three years. This turned out to be a very wise decision.

During one early-morning ritualistic physical training formation, I stood outside the front of the barracks waiting to get on with the exercises. Other members of TMC 15 with whom I worked filed passed me one by one and congratulated me on my new orders.

"Orders, what orders?" I asked.

"You're going to Berlin," one of them answered, while another one stated how lucky I was.

"Yeah, you're lucky, man. Most of the guys I know are going to Korea!"

Of course, I told Trena as soon as possible. This came as a relief to her because I had been contemplating another try with the Special Forces after being told by a retention sergeant major that I would not even have to start over, but that I could resume with the eight-week medical lab portion, just prior to phase three, where I left off before voluntarily terminating the course. Trena's encouragement, along with the advice of my superiors, convinced me that deploying to Germany was the way to go and that I should forget about the Special Forces once and for all.

During this time, Trena also informed me that we were expecting our second child, who was due shortly after our planned arrival in Berlin. Although we were thrilled about the new addition to our family, Trena naturally was not too excited that the baby's arrival was so closely tied to a major move of household goods to an overseas location.

Initially, I would have to go there alone and procure housing. The date was set for May of 1984 with the intention of coming back to bring the rest of my family soon afterward. Trena was three months away from scheduled delivery, and Aaron was nearly two years old.

CHAPTER 8

BEHIND THE WALL
EAST AND WEST BERLIN
1984-1987

One wintry night in West Berlin, my breath in front of me was like a puff of smoke as it hit the cold, icy air. It was in December 1987. I was waiting to meet my contact, who I will call Alex, on Friedrichstraße, a shopping district in West Berlin. I was to wait in front of a previously designated spot in front of a cathedral. Alex, in his early forties, and I met at Checkpoint Bravo more than a year earlier.

In August 1986, I was approached by Alex at Checkpoint Bravo while attempting to travel to the West. After numerous attempts to encourage a future meeting in East Berlin, I finally took down the information he gave me with the intention of reporting the encounter to the US intelligence community, which I did the following day.

After a long, drawn-out session with American intelligence officers to provide all the facts, they offered me a proposal, asking if I would go ahead with the meeting in East Berlin then report back everything that the Russian had in mind. At first I felt unsure about the idea but went along with their suggestion, feeling that if nothing else, it was my patriotic duty. I met with the Russian on the prearranged day and on several more occasions thereafter. This series of meetings lasted several months, until the time I left the army for college in March 1987.

Nine months later, while attending college with the support of another US agency, I was sent back to Berlin, alone, to continue these monitored meetings. The moment had arrived; I left my hotel, and walked through the blistering cold, arriving at the designated entrance. I was standing alone while throngs of people milled about the sidewalks, stopping now and then at the wooden shacks along the Kurfürstendamm to purchase Christmas items or to sip the warm tingling Gluvine.

Glancing at my watch, I noticed being a bit early. I headed down the walkway looking for a stand selling Gluvine, finding one not far away. I purchased the hot liquid, and after a few sips felt five degrees warmer. When finished, I headed back toward the church.

On my way back, I spotted Alex in the street, standing behind one of the vendor stands. He stood five feet eight and was stocky but not what I would consider obese. His hair, covered by a military-style Ushanka hat, was thick and black, styled-cut nicely. His eyes were dark as he squinted, but his genial smile kept him from looking too sinister. Alex was looking in the direction where I was supposed to be standing and seemed to be a bit fidgety.

There are moments in life when the little schoolboy rises up inside. I had one of those moments. Drawing upon all my amateur stealth training, I nonchalantly walked up behind Alex and whispered, "Hello, my friend."

The startled Russian nearly jumped out of his skin. Within a moment, he was back under control and while still looking away said, "Come on, and don't talk to me right now. Just follow me." Then, without looking back to see if I was following, immediately set off down the street.

So, we are fully in the spy mode, I surmised as I waited a few moments for the stocky Russian to get a small lead, then sauntered off after him. The street and sidewalk traffic were not too intense, so it was not difficult to keep Alex in sight. I knew that at some point we would end up in a nice, warm building somewhere.

We walked briskly through the crowds to the Friedrichstraße station, a western transfer point between several S-Bahn lines located in East Berlin territory. Although Western passengers could walk from one platform to another without ever leaving the station or needing to show papers, I was not permitted to be anywhere near there when I was assigned to the Berlin Brigade as an enlisted medic from 1984 through March 1987. It was at this moment when

I first realized that I would be going into no-man's-land on my own. Until then, I was under the impression that my meetings would be in the friendly territory of West Berlin.

Alex did not speak to me until we were on the East side, then he gave me a friendly welcome, asking me how I've been and how my wife, Trena, was doing. They met briefly in October 1986 during a prearranged dinner along with Alex's wife. No business was discussed while on the train, and when we came to one of the stops, he said, "This is where we get off. Just stay close to me and don't say anything." Feeling a little anxious, I gladly obliged.

We walked onto an icy, snowy platform with many people still milling about and headed straight toward the station. I followed him quickly down the concrete steps and was confronted by several Russian guards. Perhaps sensing my nervousness, Alex quickly spoke to them in a commanding yet pleasant voice; they said something back, sounding much like a greeting or acknowledgment. They were all smiling, a couple laughing nervously.

I continued to follow Alex outside to an waiting car, which appeared to be a new midengine Lada Samara, which at the time was only sold in Russia or to agencies for use as a pursuit vehicle. Most likely it was turbocharged with a 16-valve 300 hp engine. Bleak darkness was my first impression of this section of East Berlin outside the station. I had been traveling—without much sleep—for about thirty hours from Florida to London to Berlin.

A man sporting glasses and the same type of hat that Alex was wearing waited with the car engine running. He appeared to be a slight bit younger than Alex but was taller at six feet one. We quickly entered the car and sped off into the night. I had no idea where I was exactly. We turned onto streets that were narrow, surrounded on both sides by looming sentinel walls of brown and gray stone dilapidated buildings. The driver took the most obscure back roads possible to reach our destination . . . unknown. I did not see the familiar bustling, modern buildings surrounding Alexander Platz anywhere. The portion of East Berlin that I was being rushed through was dark and dreary, where cars and electricity seem like a pretense. The night seemed darker than before; the absence of light giving way to a massive black hole.

Far from the steel structures of Potsdamer Platz, I was in a tumultuous, distinct neighborhood consisting of abandoned buildings, derelict streets, piles of rubble, and buildings reminiscent of World War II. None of the street corners contained the characteristic Ampelmannchen on the pedestrian traffic lights. There was a dark-toned, clammy atmosphere to these chilly, dark streets.

Combined with the drive in darkness, there was an increasingly dense fog creeping in like a damp blanket. Intermittent street lamps cast dim lights between street crossings onto the wet streets. The tires rolled over cobblestones as we continued to pass narrow, dank alleys and gothic stone buildings. The streets were eerily quiet. The sky was pitch black, releasing sleet mixed with snow, and I tried not to shiver, even while traveling in a comfortably heated car. The rhythmic beating of windshield wipers drummed in my ears.

Our ride had been totally devoid of human contact until the monotony was suddenly changed by the appearance of headlights shining closer and closer behind us. This new sign of life immediately captured the undivided attention of both the driver and Alex. Not appearing to be too rattled, the two men conversed in Russian, and the driver took rapid and evasive driving techniques through the slippery, narrow streets. Startled, I asked if everything was okay. My friend assured me that it would be fine, very soon. I tried not to appear too alarmed.

He was right. After a few quick maneuvers, we lost sight of the vehicle, an expected outcome when matching a Lada Samara against an East German Trabant, built with Duroplast, a durable form of plastic containing resin strengthened by recycled wool or cotton. These cars were fueled by lifting the hood and filling a six-gallon gas tank, which then had to be mixed with two-stroke oil.

We finally arrived to our destination and emerged from the darkness back into civilization. A series of low-rise apartments surrounded us; it seemed that we were near the Karl Marx Allee area, but I was uncertain. A rusty iron fence surrounded the small park beside the apartment complex where the play area was deserted, broken, and covered partially with snow. The sky was still dark and overcast.

When I got out of the car, I immediately felt the cool, brisk, wintry winds pounding at my face. Snow flurries spun and danced around us as if led by a spirit. Before me stood a ten-story building, fronted with glass doors. Alex introduced me to Sergi, the driver. The three of us scurried up the steps to the glass-door entrance. As I battled my way toward the entrance, my cheeks and ears were slowly turning red and beginning to feel a little numb. Once inside, we took an old elevator to the ninth floor. The elevator bell rang as it stopped; the doors slowly opened.

We walked straight to a door, which Sergi unlocked and opened with a creak. Darkness filled the room until Sergi flipped on the light switch, which revealed a modest décor that impressed but did not surprise me. I glanced out the front window as we passed a small corridor toward the living room. Outside, the trees bent in submission to the howling wind.

The ceilings were plain, and the rooms contained what I pictured to be a normal amount of windows and doors by American standards. The walls were not cracked but seemed freshly painted and clean. There were no broken light bulbs dangling from the ceiling; instead, the complex was brightly lit with modern lamps and lampshades. I wondered if there was anybody else hiding somewhere in the apartment.

Alex asked me kindly to have a seat in one of the comfortable sofas and offered me some refreshments. I asked for something to drink, and he had Sergi bring me a coke. We continued small talk until Sergi brought my drink and then sat down. We began discussing the nature of our business. With a closer look at Sergi, I noticed that he had light brown, thin, wispy hair. It was clear who would be leading the discussions. My friend, Alex, no doubt was in charge of the mission.

I secretly wondered if I had fallen into a trap and was completely cut off from my world—isolated. The setting was awkward for me, but I tried my best to remain cool, attentive, and interested. Alex was jovial and light-hearted from the time we met at the Ku'damm, just as I remembered him to be. I did not feel threatened, fearful, or uneasy, but I did feel a bit apprehensive, cautious, and watchful.

Conducting spy business was straightforward. There was no other person in the apartment, relieving me of the apprehension

I felt about an enticing female agent appearing at any moment, leaving me in an awful predicament. I was warned about such measures in prior briefings with the Americans.

More than halfway through my drink, I did not feel any sleepier, so I must not have been drugged. I heard about that also but couldn't remember if that fact was from a novel. Alex was quite cordial and simply wanted me to understand the method of our future communication.

I was intrigued when he pulled out a peculiar looking pen, several prewritten letters in German, (international envelopes addressed from a German girl to another German girl in East Berlin), a book, and a set of instructions on a thin piece of microfilm. Sergi laid the materials down in front of me on a large coffee table. Then he explained what each item was and the proper procedure to use them. The whole idea was to send messages from the United States on back of the prewritten letters between two college-aged girls in invisible ink! Are they serious, I wondered? I thought that this kind of stuff was only in novels and movies.

Alex and Sergi were quite serious. They had me practice writing with my hand resting on the hardcover book. In no way was I to touch any part of the paper. I jotted some words down, what they told me to, and Sergi then disappeared to another room for a few moments.

It was then that I nervously asked Alex if the three of us were alone and if I would be going back to West Berlin that evening. "Of course we are alone, and, yes, you will go back to your hotel, Alex answered. "Why do you ask?"

"I don't know," I replied. I did not know how to answer, so I sheepishly asked, "These girls in the letters are not real, right?"

"No, we would not do anything like that to you!" Alex seemed hurt and puzzled by my question. Then I was further embarrassed when he added, "Trena is a good lady. You need to keep her."

I quickly replied, "Yes! I am glad these girls are not real!"

Alex smiled and seemed satisfied with my reply. Before the conversation could go any further, Sergi returned and said something to Alex in Russian. Alex told me that I needed to write again but to press down harder with the pen. So I went through the process a second time, and Sergi quickly disappeared to the backroom where he had gone before.

Berlin—1986

It had been almost a year when, during one of my trips to the East, that Alex asked me to bring along my wife the next time we met and have dinner together with his. "We'll have, as you might say, a double date," he said, chuckling.

His request unnerved me a bit, but I did not want to show any alarm. "Sure, sounds good. I'll ask her to come with me the next time we meet."

The two American agents, who were always seen together like Abbott and Costello, didn't act as if it was a big deal for Trena to go with me, and I wondered what they knew that I didn't. Ultimately, they left the decision up to Trena and me.

"What are these guys up to?" Trena inquired. "If you say it will be all right, I'll go."

"They assured me that nothing would happen," I said, wondering silently if they could make such assurances.

Trena agreed to go to the East with me, which meant that she would need to be briefed beforehand by the Americans.

It was a sunny day but cold with snow still on the ground when Trena joined me on a mission to the East. We parked where instructed, met the Russian, and then were ushered into his waiting car. I noticed another watching us. He was looking intently at his engine with both the vehicle's hood and trunk raised open.

"So, you are Trena. Very nice to meet you. Your husband speaks very well of you. My name is Alex."

"Yes, I'm Trena; nice to meet you."

"We will drive to the restaurant, and my wife will meet us there. She doesn't speak any English so I will have to translate."

Alex drove us to a nice restaurant along the River Spree (pronounced shpray). Both of us were quite surprised when we spotted small sailboats docked along the banks. We had a pleasant view of the nicer part of East Berlin on this rare sunny day.

Alex's wife met us at the entrance of the restaurant, and we all exchanged greetings as he introduced her as Luva. We were seated in a main open room with several other families present. Enjoying a good portion of some kind of fish dish, we mingled our eating with personal talk.

Alex's wife was a petite blonde lady who wore her hair short and looked every bit of a lady in her midforties. I had the impression that she really was uncomfortable about being there, yet she conducted herself with dignity.

At dinner, we got to know each other beyond the polite formalities. It was during this time that I discovered that Alex's grandmother used to teach him about God when he was a small child. I clearly remember when Alex, a staunch communist, said, "Maybe 5 percent of me believes that there is a God."

The afternoon meal lasted slightly less than two hours and then Luva spoke some words in Russian to Alex, who then kissed her good-bye just before she told Trena and me good-bye and departed across the busy street. Alex explained that she had to leave for a previous engagement.

Alex then took us outside of East Berlin into Potsdam, a forbidden place for US soldiers, and after pulling off the side of the road in an open field covered with snow, I knew from prior planning, that this was where I had to change from my uniform into my civilian clothes that I had brought along with me.

Trena was distraught when she mentioned the need for a lady's room and was told by the Soviet that there were no facilities anywhere nearby and that it was okay to go behind the bushes. She contemplated the situation for several moments before disappearing into the snow-covered thicket.

After piling back into Alex's car, we continued our trip, visiting several museums and taking a walk around the town. It was during these moments that Alex, knowing that I was about to depart Berlin for college, laid out his long-term plans for me.

He wanted me to become an officer in the military intelligence and arrange an assignment back to Berlin or to another location in Germany. I listened with interest, taking in all of his words, knowing that I would later be debriefed by the Americans.

When the day was complete, we made another field stop, where I changed back into my uniform and then the three of us headed back to where my car was parked. Trena and I needed to get back across Checkpoint Charley before curfew. The sunny afternoon was rapidly changing into a cloudy, misty evening. The temperature dropped, turning the night cold and blustery, accented by the snow stacked up along dreary streets.

Trena and I thanked our gracious host for a wonderful day. We got into our mustard-colored Opel in a hurry, needing to cross Checkpoint Charley before curfew. I turned the ignition key in the rapidly declining blistering cold. There was no sound. "Dead!" I uttered, a bit worried. "The battery is dead." The clock was ticking. Our kids were in the West; Trena and I were stuck in the East

"Aaaagh, you've got to be kidding!" Trena snapped. Her first and only trip to East Berlin during a meeting with a Soviet officer, the car was dead, and her kids were home. Alex suddenly appeared at her window.

"Not to worry. Trena, you have driven this before, yes?"

"Oh, yeah, I can drive it."

"Good; you sit at the wheel while Scott and I go to the back and shove. You will keep the car in neutral, and when I say, 'Now,' you let up the clutch. You can do that?"

"No problem! Of course I can do it," Trena replied nervously.

I got out of the car, and Trena took the wheel. Alex gave me a big smile as we leaned on the trunk. I could tell that he thought well of Trena because of his pleasant manner toward her and his numerous compliments.

"Are you guys ready?' she yelled.

"Yes!" Alex answered back. "Go!"

Set in neutral, the car slowly rolled forward as Alex and I pushed, our feet slipping on the icy pavement as we tried to maintain traction. Abruptly, the car jerked to a stop just as the two of us began to gain some momentum. Like tossed luggage, both of us flew up over the trunk into the back windshield then rolled off on either side onto the wet snow.

Jumping up quickly while brushing off the snow from our coats, we speedily approached Trena, who was doubled over with hysterical laughter, trying to form the words, "Are you guys all right?"

"What were you doing?" Alex interjected before I could even open my mouth. "I thought you knew how to do this. What was that?" he continued incredulously.

Trena was still speechless from her fit of laughter. "I . . . I'm so sorry!" she said, coughing back the laughter.

"Okay, listen to me now! This is what you must do," Alex began, but Trena held up her hands while choking.

"I got it now; I promise! My foot slipped," she said, trying to sound serious.

Alex looked at me, and I just shrugged my shoulders trying not to be too aggravated. Looking at Trena, I decided to weigh in. "Hey, babe, are you sure you know what you're doing?"

"Yes, Scott, I'm sure. Go on back there and try again," she managed testily between her laughs.

We went to the back, laying our hands on the trunk, while still hearing Trena enjoy herself from the front. Alex looked over at me with the helpless eyes of surrender. Then he shook his head in wonderment.

"Women!" he muttered.

It was my turn to burst into laughter. Alex joined me. The two of us with all our differences discovered a universal common bond, and both of us shared the moment, a primal understanding of a more ancient and eternal conflict, that of the husband and wife.

And with that, we pushed again. Trena got it right this time, waiting until the Opel had reached sufficient speed before popping the clutch. Her efforts were met with the roar of the engine coming to life. *Thank God!*

Berlin—1987

Nearly a year later, at the apartment, Alex spoke first and laid out the plan for the next day in East Berlin. He talked excitedly about the museums we would visit and the restaurant he wanted to take me to afterward for dinner. He wanted to, as he said, "Enjoy our moment together, just like old times."

I remembered all the vodka he ordered during our first meeting in 1986. He had a shot as an appetizer and then one with his salad, his dinner, his dessert, and after-dessert coffee. He also needed an extra one to put into his coffee. Of course, I was to join him with each. That made for an interesting afternoon trying to get back into the West side through Checkpoint Charley.

Fortunately, two plainclothes young men in long overcoats directed me through the MP guard to a parking lot. While one of them looked through the front of my car, the other, a five-feet-eleven man with short, cropped blond hair, had me open my trunk and, while briefly looking inside, said, "How did everything go?"

The reason for this visit, more than a year later and after I got out of the army (the first time), was to reestablish contact and to begin this new communication method. Alex also wanted to check on my progress of becoming an officer in the military intelligence field. At the time, I could only tell him that I was successful in getting into an ROTC program, which was an officer training corps at the university level. He understood.

Sergi emerged again, this time with a smile, thumbs-up and a "Да!" Alex smiled also.

"Okay, you are ready, my friend. Let's get you back to the train so you can go back to the hotel. You must be tired."

"Yes, I am," I answered.

The three of us left the apartment, entered the Lada Samara, and then sped off into the snowy night, back to the train station. Alex walked with me up the platform steps past the fewer Russian guards and waited for the S-Bhan train until it clattered to a halt. After reminding me of our same meeting place on Friedrichstraße and set time for the next morning, I boarded the rear car and headed back to the West, trying not to look too conspicuous. Mentally, I sensed the staring eyes from the other passengers as if I had an American flag sewn on my jacket, which of course I did not for the obvious reasons.

As the train rambled down the tracks, the song by Tears for Fears, "Everybody Wants to Rule the World," came to mind. *Welcome to your life. There's no turning back*

I stopped often on my way back to the hotel, acting like I was interested in my surroundings, like a tourist. Inside of me, I felt a little paranoid in reality; I was attempting to detect any particular individual who appeared to be watching or following me.

Sheer relief swept over me when I arrived back to the hotel without incident. The first time all night I could breathe normally. There was one more thing I needed to do before calling it a night. I prayed, thanking God, pulled out a brand new Bible that I brought over with me, and wrote some inspiring verses in the front blank portion. Then I finally turned off the lights and fell right to sleep.

The following morning was crisp, the sun poking through the gliding smoke-colored clouds. Alex had me meet him in a slightly different location on Friedrichstraße, closer to the S-Bahn station. The first contact routine was the same, a visual acknowledgment followed by a five to ten meter distance following until we were in East Berlin. Nobody seemed to be paying particular attention to us throughout the ride. We exited the train onto the same platform as the previous night. Only about three Soviet guards were at the bottom of the steps.

Sergei was waiting for us with the Lada Samara's engine running. The interior was nice and warm. This time, we did not weave through back streets but instead went toward the center of East Berlin. It was nearing the lunch hour, with breakfast being my own responsibility at the hotel.

Alex and I were left off at the end if a long, winding sidewalk leading through a park. "This is Treptower Park!" he announced proudly.

Treptower was a popular park located along the river Spree in the Treptow-Köpenick district. Besides having a Soviet war memorial, it contained a military cemetery that commemorated five thousand of the eighty thousand Soviet soldiers who fell in the Battle of Berlin in April and May 1945. It opened four years after the war ended, on May 8, 1949. Not long after President Reagan gave his famous speech, "Mr. Gorbachev, tear down this wall," the park was used for a rock concert by the British Rock Band Barclay James Harvest on July 14, 1987. It marked the first-ever open-air concert by a Western rock band in the German Democratic Republic.

A small, brown, wooden shack stood along the walkway about one hundred meters from where we were. Across from it was a park bench. A man in his early sixties was in the stand behind a counter containing several food items to choose from. Alex and I had some steamy currywurst, one of the traditional snacks in the area. The white-haired man served us the sliced pork sausage swimming in a curry-tomato sauce and gave us each some white bread to go with it.

Sauntering over to the park bench, we observed a young couple pushing a stroller with an eighteen-month-old, all bundled up from the cold. Based on the color of the clothes and buggy, I assumed the baby was a boy. The couple glanced at us briefly but moved along without altering their pace.

Alex reviewed the procedures with me from the previous evening concerning the invisible letters. I chuckled a bit, and every time that I did so, he replied, "You must not laugh. Why? Because . . ." and then he would proceed to explain why I shouldn't be laughing. He wanted me to make sure that I believed him when he explained how prosperous I could be if everything went according to plan.

I replied that I wasn't really laughing but was simply overwhelmed by this whole experience. He understood, or so he said. After we finished eating, we walked a little farther so that Alex could show me the Soviet war memorial.

Our brief meeting on the park bench was followed by a drive through the city and to Potsdam's Museum *Im Güldenen Arm*, a baroque-style building that dominated during the reign of Frederick William I. The museum's exhibition included civil development, documents of the garrison period, and special exhibitions on Potsdam's history. We spent a few hours here.

Berlin—1986

A lot had changed since my first meeting with Alex nearly a year before. I finished my enlistment service time of seven years, became a civilian, and began college and the ROTC program in Lakeland, Florida. Trena had supported my decision. Alex once shared with me, while in Potsdam, that I should become a military intelligence officer and try to get an assignment in Germany.

The American military intelligence handlers made arrangements for me to be "handed over" to the FBI, since I would now be a civilian during the transition. They felt that if I was willing, this plan could be a breakthrough for the Americans as well. "We can't make you or tell you what to do, but if your plan has been all along to go through ROTC and become a military intelligence officer, that would be great!"

During my first encounter with the FBI, I was introduced to two agents. We met in Clearwater, Florida, at the pier. Only one of them, Bart*, would turn out to be my contact. He would drive to Lakeland once a month from Tampa and meet with me for lunch. I agreed to have my phone tapped with a recording device, since Alex's plan to keep in touch would be through an inventive use of international telephone communication.

One afternoon, while studying my college courses, I received a call from Alex. The voice was faint, but I could still understand him. I quickly flipped on the recorder once I knew it was him. He wanted me to come to East Berlin for a meeting. "It would be wonderful if you could visit me again, soon," Alex had pressed during one call. "There are many things we should talk about."

"It would be great to see you again, Alex. But travel to Europe is expensive, and I am going to college now. Hmmm. I wonder . . ." I replied as my mind quickly processed all the options facing me.

The FBI mentioned before that they would support such a trip. But it was imperative that Alex not suspect that I was working for the Feds. "You know, I think my grandfather might help with the airfare. He wanted some items that I failed to bring back the first time."

"That's great!" Alex exclaimed. "Yes, see if he will help you, and maybe we can help also if you come."

Immediately after receiving a call from Alex, my previous instructions directed me to drive to a nearby phone booth and contact Bart to let him know that we had made contact. Bart would then travel the following day to Lakeland.

I excitedly drove to a local Texaco station, the closest place with a public phone, but noticed that a man was staring inside the hood of his car. His trunk was wide open as well, and although the chances of something being fishy were unlikely, I continued to drive through the parking lot and sought another public phone elsewhere.

Bart was excited about the contact and quickly made arrangements to meet the following day. Soon afterward, arrangements were made for the visit to East Berlin. Trena was not very comfortable about me going to East Berlin alone even though she had met and liked Alex.

I really wasn't comfortable, for that matter, either. However, Bart liked the idea and said the FBI would fund the entire trip. But money was one thing; available assets in Germany was quite another.

The FBI operated primarily in the United States. They had no plans; at least to my knowledge, of being anywhere near Berlin to support me if something unexpected happened. Bart assured me that everything would work out and that I would not have to go if I didn't feel comfortable with it. 'Yeah, right,' I thought. I was already in this too deep.

The Americans had their agenda; the Soviets had theirs, and unknown to any of us, God had his. I knew that I was merely a pawn in this international game of political intrigue. "Maybe 5 percent of me believes in a God," Alex had told me over dinner a year ago. My missionary roots were slowly rising to the surface.

I was willing to be a pawn in their espionage game to help with a higher American cause. Whatever and whosever's agenda this next meeting concerned, it was about to be played out on this cold, wintery day in December 1987.

Berlin—1987

It was starting to get dark as five o'clock approached during the winter month of December. I remembered that during the summer month of July, it was quite the opposite, with the sun rising around five thirty and setting around ten thirty.

"Are you getting hungry?" Alex asked.

"Yes, I am."

Our pace picked up, and we made our way to the waiting Lada. Alex said something to Sergei in Russian, and he replied, "Да!" We drove back through the city, talking about anything, everything, and nothing. Then Sergei let us off at a familiar place. It was Hotel Moskau in Karl Marx Allee. This was one restaurant at which Americans were allowed to eat whenever they traveled to the East. I was a bit apprehensive that I would run into somebody that I knew until the two of us were quickly ushered to a different section of the restaurant that I had not seen before. It was decorated nicely and was surrounded by thick red curtains. Alex and I had the whole room and long table for ourselves.

Sitting across the table from Alex, I realized that I had once regarded him as an archenemy. But I had met the enemy face-to-face and had discovered that the enemy was just a man not much unlike me.

During my seven years in the army I had been indoctrinated to despise the Russians, and yet here I was sitting down to cordially share a meal with a Russian officer. The irony struck me personally because I inwardly knew the KGB shared the blame, as did the Colombian terrorists, for the devastation caused by their violent activities.

"I will prepare a table before you in the presence of your enemies" (Psalm 23:5). I thought about this verse as it came to life.

Despite the fact that sinister KGB officers probably committed horrendous acts and represented the most despicable and ruthless forms of communism, I, nonetheless, felt quite comfortable talking with Alex and felt no ill will toward this man.

Alex was, in fact, quite polished, educated, and polite, and acted more civil than many of the Americans I had encountered. Our talk this night strayed far from business and drifted off into our own ways of life. Alex spoke sadly of the extended Russian involvement in Afghanistan. We discussed the ongoing war between Iran and Iraq and its implications for the future.

"Your country and ours are so much alike. We will continue to go the same course together against our common enemies." Alex repeated a conversation we'd had the year before. "As you know, we were allies during WWII. Even now, our leaders are good friends, Mr. Gorbachev and your president, Reagan."

The food smelled delicious as three waiters laid the plates in front of us . . . along with two new shot glasses of vodka. We ate, talked in between bites, and enjoyed a typical social meal without any mention as to why I was there or what he was wanting from me. I was a bit surprised, but the situation allowed me to act natural more easily. The food, a five-course meal, with vodka, served by four waiters, was very delicious. It seemed to be a combined Cornish hen with a small beef rump smothered in some sort of wine sauce. Our conversation centered on social and political topics, carefully avoiding anything to do with the business at hand.

Our main dish came while we were busy discussing world events, the situation in Afghanistan with their troops and the clash between Iran and Iraq. At one point in our conversation, Alex added, "We are much alike, just as we were during World War II. We were allies then and should be again soon. Our real enemies are those terrorists in the Middle East. We should be fighting them together."

Throughout the meal, I looked for an opportunity to tell Alex that I had a special gift for him in the car with our bags. That moment came when things were quiet, and we waited for the bill. Alex had a gratifying look on his face, as if he had just finished a feast.

"Alex, do you remember last year when we were together with our wives, and you told everyone that maybe 5 percent of you believed in a God because your grandmother taught you when you were six years old?"

He smiled, "Yes, of course. But I can't believe that you remembered."

"Yes, I do, and I have something to give you that your grandmother would want you to have."

"That is very kind of you. I shall look forward to receiving this."

Shortly afterward, we turned in our tokens at the desk to retrieve our winter coats and then went out the front door, where Sergei was waiting for us, engine running, the interior nice and warm. On our way to the S-Bahn station, where I would say my farewell to Alex and head back to the West and then to the United States the following day, I pulled the new hardcover NIV Bible out of my bag. Then I held it out toward Alex and said, "This is what your grandmother would want you to have."

Alex appeared deeply moved as he clutched the green-colored Bible with both hands. Then he looked at the cover, held it up to his chest and said, "Thank you very much. I always wanted one of these to read."

Alex placed the Bible in his bag and pulled a Russian book out for me in another gift exchange. When Sergei dropped us off near the S-Bahn station, Alex took me inside a small shop before moving toward the stairwell. It was a quaint little shop with a variety of knickknacks. Alex pointed out a few pieces of china that were setting against the back wall.

"Do you like any of those china sets?"

"They are all nice," I replied.

"Which do you like the best?"

I pointed one out and said, "That one looks especially artistic."

The next thing I knew, Alex was purchasing the set and had it boxed and tied together with string. Alex grabbed the box from the gray-haired woman in her midsixties and exchanged a few words with her. Then we darted out the door and up the stairs past the young Soviet guards and onto the snow-covered platform. The flurries were coming down harder as the evening wore on. We stood together until the rickety train clanked down the tracks from the east.

As it approached the platform where we were standing, Alex handed me the box and said, "Please give this to Trena from me."

"Thank you very much, Alex. I'm sure she will greatly appreciate this!"

I turned to shake his hand as the train screeched to a halt, but Alex grabbed me in a big bear-hug instead.

"Take care, my friend, and stay safe."

"Good-bye, Alex. Thank you for your hospitality today and for Trena's gift." I always knew that he was fond of her because when we all met the year before, he insisted on carrying her fireman style in front of him when we came to a large puddle of water. He did not want her to get her stylish boots wet.

"You better get aboard."

I entered the last car, placed the brown box at my feet and held onto the vertical silver pole. Then I faced outside in Alex's direction before the door closed. He remained where I left him. The train jerked forward, causing me to hold on to the pole with a tighter grip, and we began slowly moving away from the platform. Alex stood with his hands buried in his coat pockets for a brief period and then lifted one of them to wave farewell. I waved back and then looked for an empty seat.

I found one facing the front, and as I sat down, I thought I heard a voice whisper in my ear, "Well done, thy faithful servant. Mission accomplished."

I had a feeling then that I would never see Alex again. This turned out to be true. I never saw him again. Two years later, the Berlin Wall was torn down by the people, and the Soviets moved away from Berlin. It was during my last semester of college while doing an internship, teaching high school social studies at Hardee High. I told the students, "I never thought I would see this day come."

* Not their real names.

**After the wedding ceremony and leaving for honeymoon
—Salem, Virginia (1981)**

**Trena and our firstborn, Aaron
Scott—Fort Bragg, North Carolina (1983)**

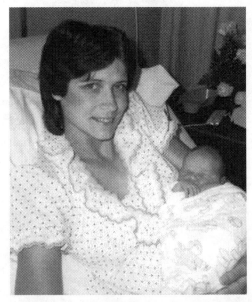

Trena with our second child, Jacquelyn Marie (1984)

The Berlin Wall—Where the East met the West (1984)

Christmas in Berlin (1985)

Jacquie's second birthday—Berlin (1986)

Part 2

Commissioned, and the War on Terror

Chapter 9

Desert Storm
Riyadh, Saudi Arabia
January 1991

Many will come from the east and the west, and will take
their places at the feast
—Matthew 8:11

Bam! Bam! Bam! Someone was pounding loudly on the room's only door. I didn't know or care who it was, but I was definitely annoyed after grabbing only two hours of sleep.

"Get into MOPP Level 1, ASAP! War has begun!" The voice on the other side yelled. I jumped up, nearly knocking over Second Lieutenant Frank Soccha, who had jumped up from his bed across from mine. "Wow, what are we supposed to do now?" I asked groggily.

At the same time I wondered how safe we were here in the capital city of Riyadh. Somewhere in the frenzy, I glanced at my watch to make careful note of the time and date. Set on twenty-four-hour time, my watch glowed 0320 as I pushed the little button with which I had changed the reading the previous evening to reflect the local time. The date lit up as well—*TH 1-17*.

MOPP (mission oriented protective posture-level 1) was the signal for donning the overgarments, jacket, and pants for protective measures against a chemical or biological attack.

The levels began at 1 and ran up to 4, with 4 being the severest threat and requiring that a soldier be covered from head to toe with the mask, overgarments, boots, and gloves. Although the mask was also put on during MOPP level 3, I quickly discovered that when Scud missiles launched from Iraq approached Riyadh (which was frequently), levels 1 and 2 were often skipped and the mask was the first item utilized.

Frank and I walked out into the main living room of the villa, which was located outside of Riyadh in a compound designed for Bedouins called Eskan Village. Containing nearly 850 villas, this base was the primary housing area for American troops arriving in droves to face Saddam's army, the fourth largest army in the world.

I noticed several other men also dressed in protective gear standing around a TV set showing the coalition aircraft bombing of Baghdad that just had taken place. Actually, no aircraft were involved in the bombing, just surface-to-air missiles lighting up the Baghdad sky, with much of the surface aglow with flames.

As everybody was adding their two cents' worth of what was going to happen next, some soldiers slowly approached me and introduced themselves. I couldn't remember all of their names, but I quickly realized that I was outranked by all of them except Frank.

Five other captains were sharing the same villa, which was equipped with a large living room, small dining area, large kitchen, five bedrooms, and three bathrooms. A stairway led up to the flat roof exposed to the Saudi sky.

Arriving late the night before, after traveling at least twenty-four hours on a C-5 Galaxy that had originated at Pope Air Force Base (AFB), North Carolina, I was assigned to my room at 0100. I had made stops at an AFB in Massachusetts and Madrid, Spain, before landing in Dhahran, Saudi Arabia.

When I, along with a line of other soldiers, filed out of the air-conditioned jet, M-16s in hand, we were immediately engulfed by the arid heat of Saudi Arabia. All around me I took note of the numerous American aircraft, pallets loaded down with supplies and personal gear, and soldiers milling about seemingly with a purpose and direction.

Only five months had elapsed since the first wave of American soldiers from the Second Brigade, Eighty-Second Division Airborne had landed at the airfield. Armed with approximately forty thousand troops, M55 Sheridan tanks, and AH-64 Apache helicopters, they figured their role to be only a buffer and were prepared to act as a speed bump if Saddam continued with his massive force into Saudi Arabia.

I started to wander, hoping to locate the next line of processing that would get me quickly to my next destination, in Riyadh. There, I would meet up with my unit for the first time.

The tiring trip was too long, in my opinion, and I reflected back painfully on how and why I was back in the army after leaving it once before and how I had left behind Trena, Aaron, and Jacquie, who were now eight and six, respectively.

I had departed from home at the extremely early morning hour of two o'clock and was taken to the Green Ramp on Pope Air Force Base by my parents.

Green Ramp, the site of many previous prejump exercises, was the departing location, where we would load onto a C-5 Galaxy jet aircraft en route to the war in the Middle East. The night before was one of the worse nights that I could remember in a long, long time.

Earlier, while loading my duffle bag full of military gear, I was well aware that four little eyes were watching quietly from behind me. The days were going by fast. Soon, I would leave my family behind and depart for Saudi Arabia.

I tried to make light of the unfolding situation and grabbed my protective mask and threw it over my face. In one swift motion, I turned quickly toward Aaron and Jacquie, lifted my arms wide, and growled like a bear. Though responding with laughter and a feeble attempt to get away, their attention was riveted on the mask itself.

"Will you have to wear that in war?" Aaron asked quizzically.

Uh-oh, I thought. *Here we go.*

"I hope not," I finally replied.

"What's it for?" Jacquie inserted quickly.

"Well, just for added protection . . ." I began before being interrupted by Aaron.

"In case Saddam uses chemical gas against you," he added with a mixture of knowledge and concern.

"What kind of gas?" Jacquie asked in a panic.

Before I could answer, Trena put a stop to the conversation by informing them that dinner was ready and that she could use some big helpers to set the table.

"Go on and help Mommy now," I encouraged them, trying not to sound choked up.

It helped that my parents were also present, having flown up from Colombia after receiving the news that I would soon be deployed to Saudi Arabia. Dad continued the conversation where Aaron and Jacquie had left off.

A few hours later, I said my courageous good-byes—there would be time for tears later—and reminded them to pray for Daddy and that I would be back soon. With four hours of waiting time before departure, I again thought back over the previous years that had led me to this point.

After leaving Berlin, and the army, for that matter, I began college and was finished within two years. I graduated with a bachelor's degree in education and also finished ROTC in late 1989. My performance during the summer Advanced Camp at Fort Riley, Kansas, in 1988 was better than I had anticipated. Because of that success, I was encouraged and eventually selected to return to the regular army, this time as a part of the Military Intelligence Branch.

In the spring of 1990, I reported to Fort Huachuca, Arizona, to begin my Officer Basic Course. Located just outside of Sierra Vista and seventy miles southeast of Tucson, I procured housing before Trena and the kids joined me. Classes started on the first of June and lasted six months.

Set in the rugged southwest mountains, which glowed violet and orange at dusk, we became quite comfortable with our new laid-back lifestyle in a military community setting. There were a couple of officers in my class who, like me, had prior service time as an enlisted soldier. We quickly formed friendships together though I was the oldest of them and the only one in the class with children in school.

These were good times for our whole family because I was starting a fresh career where the paycheck was stable, and I was no longer a full-time student. Becoming a military officer had been a topic of discussion and a dream very early in our marriage. It came to reality just a year after the Berlin Wall came crumbling down. When I was stationed in Berlin, I could only dream about becoming a commissioned officer.

Only two months had gone by since I had reentered the army and had begun attending intelligence courses when Saddam Hussein decided to invade Kuwait. President George Bush was determined to draw a line in the sand and kick him out.

We were given access to classified briefings on the assessment of the enemy. The instructors' words echoed in my head after all the numbers were crunched. "It's going to be bloody," they informed us.

Not long after the Eighty-Second Airborne and other units began filtering into Saudi Arabia, I learned where my next assignment would be. All of us students were handed, one-by-one, our new duty assignments written on a new set of orders.

At the top of the paper, between two emblems, one of which was the army seal, the words, DEPARTMENT OF THE ARMY were written with an address immediately below it. Two lines below were the ORDERS, number, and date. Four lines below these was a line with a soldier's full name and Social Security number listed. Then the paragraph began:

You are assigned to Fourth Psychological Operations Group (Airborne), Fort Bragg, North Carolina.

Reporting Date: 17 December 1990.

I didn't need to look further for any more details. I already knew what it meant. The Fourth PSYOP Group was the only active psychological operations unit in the army. Its mission was to deploy anywhere in the world on short notice, to plan, develop, and conduct civil affairs and psychological operations in support of coalition forces or other government agencies as directed by the National Command Authority. Most of the unit, I would soon discover, was already in Saudi Arabia.

How am I going to break the news to Trena? I wondered. *And the kids.*

"What are you stressing over?" Ron Misak asked me. He had served in the Eighty-Second Airborne as an enlisted soldier around the same time I had been stationed at Fort Bragg.

"Take a look at this," I said while handing him my orders. "I'm going back to Fort Bragg, to a Special Ops unit."

"Wow, that's good," Ron countered.

"You wanna switch assignments?" I asked incredulously.

"Sure, I'll go back there."

The trade never took place, of course, and soon our family was destined to move to North Carolina, the place Aaron was born eight years before. Trena did a convincing job of hiding her distress if she had any. Like the trooper she always was, together we left for North Carolina together with a stop at her parents' home in Roanoke, Virginia.

Thanksgiving was coming up, and I decided to drive down to Fort Bragg from Roanoke to check out my new unit in case people left early for a four-day weekend. I wanted to find out just what was in store for me when I arrived there.

The Fourth Psychological Operations Group headquarters was nearly deserted. In fact, most of Fort Bragg appeared that way to me in comparison to the last time I remembered it. I walked into the only office abuzz with activity and looked around for the officer in charge (OIC).

A sergeant walking past with a handful of papers stopped and asked, "Can I help you?"

"I'm looking for the OIC," I responded.

"That's him over there," The sergeant said, pointing across the room to a major sitting at a desk talking on the phone.

"Thanks," I said to the sergeant and then walked toward the major.

Standing in front of the husky officer's desk, I didn't want to come across as being impatient or apprehensive. I looked with interest at some of the photos and products hanging around the walls. Just then I heard the major say on the phone, "There's a lieutenant standing here in front of me right now." He looked up at me.

I returned his gaze, studying him carefully. "Yeah, I'll call you back. Let me find out what this young man needs."

The major hung up the phone, and I reached across the desk and said, "Sir, I'm Lieutenant Scott Meehan, and I have been assigned to this unit." I handed him a copy of my orders.

"Yes, we've been expecting you," he said sternly. "You've been assigned to the Eighth Battalion, and they're already gone. I need you to sign in ASAP and don't bother to unpack."

I acted like his words didn't faze me at all and acknowledged an affirmation as the sergeant I had spoken to earlier was called back with the instructions to take me down to the battalion.

"Do you want to sign in now?" the sergeant asked me.

"Negative. Not yet," I answered, low enough so that the major wouldn't hear.

"Roger that!" the sergeant said, smiling. "Come on. I'll take you down to battalion."

"Let's go."

Whoever was supposed to be there must have been out to lunch. The front door to the building was locked.

"I guess you can come back after lunch," the sergeant said. "Will you need me then?" he asked, hoping I would just say, "No."

When I did, the sergeant came to attention and saluted smartly. I returned it, hoping that when I did come back after lunch, the door would still be locked.

I decided to look up one of my former ROTC instructors who I knew had been recently assigned to Fort Bragg. Maybe we could have lunch together, I reasoned. Major Billingsly was excited to hear from one of his former students, and he quickly seized the opportunity to take me to lunch.

While eating at one of the many Chinese restaurants on Yadkin Road, I relayed the facts surrounding my hasty new assignment and the challenge it was going to be to settle my family into a new area while in the middle of a deployment.

Trying not to sound too distressed while unloading, I was glad when Major Billingsly quickly and forcefully asked me, "What's the date on your orders?"

"The seventeenth of December," I answered.

"All right, this is what you do. Go get your family, get them into a house, and get your kids into school. When you have done all of that, then, and only then, do you report in on that date, and not a day sooner."

"Okay, thanks for the advice!" I exclaimed with renewed vigor.

The four of us, along with Trena's family, enjoyed a great Thanksgiving together then headed on to Fayetteville, staying with an old SF buddy, Keith Butler, his wife, Karen, and their three boys. The tasks ahead of me would be accomplished one by one, methodically, until that day I needed to report. It wasn't long before we found a house for us to move into, and the kids were enrolled in a nearby school. We planned for an early Christmas and began our shopping in haste.

When the seventh finally came around, I went straight to the Eighth Battalion orderly room and met another major, one I had never seen before. Standing up and greeting me with an expression of happiness, the major stretched out his hand. "Hi, I'm Major Merkle. You must be the new lieutenant that Group told us to watch out for."

"Yes, sir, Scott Meehan," I answered.

I was about to volunteer the reason for not coming and signing in earlier when Major Merkle surprisingly said, "Well, you might as well relax for a while. The air force has suspended flights from here into theater until after Christmas. They won't resume again until the fourteenth of January, and we already have you manifested for the first flight out."

I wanted to shout for joy and could hardly contain my excitement, but I answered back, "Oh, that's too bad, sir. I was looking forward to getting there," wondering if the major could detect any sort of sarcasm.

Trena, Aaron, and Jacquie were elated with the news when I sprung it on them at home that afternoon. We were going to make the most and best of our remaining time together and, to top it off, actually be together for Christmas.

That first night in Riyadh came too quickly, and I found myself among follow officers standing in chemical protective gear in Saudi Arabia. We were ready and willing to do our part in facing down Saddam and his massive force along the border, yet were unsure what was in store for us down the road.

On my first full day in Riyadh, I accompanied several officers and soldiers to an SUV, and we headed downtown to the ten-story office building where the Eighth Battalion was headquartered. I learned that I would be on the night shift, monitoring incoming message traffic on intelligence from the line units.

I kept myself busy analyzing intelligent reports that were faxed in from units on the front lines. Going through each line carefully with a yellow highlighter, I would choose the relevant information for my commander, Lieutenant Colonel Jeffrey Jones, and then run my marker through the section that seemed important for their specific role in the campaign.

Next, I would consolidate the information and produce an INTSUM (intelligence summary) based on the pertinent information that I had gathered from the field. This document oftentimes gave firsthand accounts from these reports from the field derived from Iraqi defectors who were interrogated by frontline Psychological Operations soldiers and officers. It was one of the first sheets of paper that the commander picked up in the morning when he and his primary staff arrived to work at 0600 hours.

Once read, Lieutenant Colonel Jones would ask me questions for clarifications, which wasn't often, but still, I waited until the boss released me for the day along with the remaining evening shift crew so that we could make the drive back to Eskan Village, grab some breakfast at the dining facility, and then hit the hay.

On my second night there, the radio operator received a garbled voice message cackling over the radio from somewhere downrange. "Incoming your way in five mikes—minutes—over."

"Roger, out!" I heard the startled voice of Sergeant Menke. He was sitting by the window and monitoring the army satellite communications links, which included the AN/TSC-85 terminal at corps level and was linked to the division level's AN/TSC-93. The Division AN/TSC-85 in turn was linked to brigade level AN/TSC-93 terminals. The radios set up in the office where I worked contained the Motorola AN/URC-101 and AN/PRC 77 Radio Set; a manpack, portable VHF FM combat-net radio transceiver used to provide short-range, two-way radiotelephone voice communication.

Seconds later, the capital city of Riyadh reverberated with air-raid sirens echoing throughout the city.

I threw my mask on and bolted up the back stairwell following the other soldiers and officers pulling duty on the night shift. I had assumed that we were going to run downstairs to some sort of shelter. Instead, to my horror everybody took off up the stairs.

The climb from the tenth floor to the rooftop was exhausting enough but was made worse with the additional challenge of wearing the protective mask.

I thought such lunacy, running to the roof to view the Patriot missiles versus the incoming Scud rocket was something I could live without ever witnessing. However, after the soldiers told me about all the awesome firework displays after a Patriot made contact with a Scud, I decided that I had to see for myself.

The Iraqis used the Russian-made Scud B ballistic missile. Once launched, the missile would race skyward, capable of reaching suborbital heights of 94 miles, or 150 kilometers, before arching back downward toward its target on earth.

This muggy night in Riyadh echoed with air-raid sirens. It was annoying. Suddenly, like a UFO from outer space, a red streak appeared in the night sky and arched its way toward us. Then, two orange streaks raced skyward to meet the large red-trailed Scud missile arching toward the city! *Boom, boom!*

One of the Patriot antiaircraft missiles connected with the Scud. Another *boom!* Now that was a fireworks display!

Everything happened so fast. Our masks stayed on a bit longer just in case the rocket carried poisonous gases. I was impressed with the sight but not the possible outcome.

And so it went. All of us conducting night shift duty found a way to beat the boredom of manning the downtown office while most of Saudi Arabia slept.

We each had our own duties and tasks, with various methods of conducting them. One of the officers was on a determined mission to break his own record playing some sort of game on the computer called Castlevania.

"If this is the way the war is played," I reasoned, "then I can handle this." I was even able to call Trena on a frequent basis from our downtown office. Hearing her voice along with Aaron's and Jacquie's always lifted my spirits.

"Hello, boy," was the way in which Jacquie always greeted me in her tough, girlish way. Both she and Aaron talked excitedly about a new Nintendo game that "Mommy's going to get us."

Another spare time opportunity I took advantage of was to memorize Psalm 91—the soldiers psalm. These words comforted me much like Psalm 23 did when I was nearly blown up in Bogota, Colombia, fifteen years earlier.

One morning as I waited for the commander to release me, I noticed that Lieutenant Colonel Jones seemed a bit perplexed after reading a message sent to him from a major on the front lines with the marines. I even remembered the request coming in the night before from the fax machine.

"Great things happening here. I was able to convince General Boomer on his need for PSYOP assets. He wants a team put together for him ASAP. I could use an S-2 (intelligence and security staff) and S-3 (operations)."—Major Gerblick.

I watched as Lieutenant Colonel Jones handed the message to the primary intelligence/security staff officer (S-2), Captain Faruqi. After reading the note, Captain Faruqi looked up at the colonel and said, "You want me to go, sir?"

"Oh, no, you're my S-2; you're not going anywhere."

"So, you want Staff Sergeant Villanueva to go? I need h—" he began but was cut off by the commander.

"Not him either," Jones said candidly.

"Then who did you have in mind, sir?" Captain Faruqi pleaded. "I don't have . . ." as he was beginning to plead his case, Lieutenant Colonel Jones was pointing directly at me. "I think the young lieutenant here is quite capable."

"Oh, yes, sir! Great idea! I forgot all about him!" Captain Faruqi exclaimed, jumping to his feet.

This is just great, I thought to myself as both men approached to congratulate me on being chosen to carry out such an important mission.

"We'll take care of the details and make the arrangements," Lieutenant Colonel Jones added. "For now, go on back and get some sleep. We'll try to have you out of here in a couple of days."

"All right, sir, no problem. I'll be ready," I said smartly, even if I wasn't feeling that way.

The First Marine Expeditionary Force, or the Marine Air Ground Task Force (MAGTF) was primarily composed of the First Marine Division, Third Marine Aircraft Wing and First Marine Logistics Group. I would later discover that among the marines, it was common to call themselves I MEF as in "eye mef," or "first mef." The First Marine Expeditionary Force was commanded by Lieutenant General Walter Boomer.

I would have to wait until later that night during my normal time to call home before I could share the news with Trena about going to the front lines. The truth was I wouldn't be able to even disclose that fact. I thought all day on how I would "drop the bomb" about moving from my plush setting in Riyadh and not being able to talk to her again for who knew how long.

I tried not to read too deeply into the message for any hidden meaning. *I'm going to be sent where?* I asked Captain Faruqi for a copy of the note, which I then read in its entirety.

Wow, the marines! Who knows, maybe they'll change their mind. It was time to crack down and escalate my study on the soldiers' psalm.

Fayetteville, North Carolina, February 12, 1991: Trena tried hard to hold back the tears after the phone call in which I informed her of my move. "He couldn't even tell me where he was going or for how long," she cried to her mother on the phone after being sure that the kids were in bed. Trena already decided to allow neither Aaron nor Jacquie the privilege of watching the news on TV. Trena had decided this after discovering Jacquie sitting on the couch in tears and blurting out, "I don't want them to do that to Daddy!"

Looking at the set, Trena saw the parade of beaten coalition force pilots that were shot down over Iraq and made a spectacle of by Saddam's own psychological campaign.

"Daddy's going to be all right," Trena said, assuring her as she sat down next to Jacquie and put her arm around her tightly. "Keep praying, and God will watch over him."

Trena, like many wives all over the country, carried on with her life and raising the kids while her husband was off in a foreign land fighting a war. She determined that none of this was going to get the best of her, and she, along with the other wives of the unit, pulled together and supported their husbands at all costs. She's a great wife. I desired to come back home to her and watch our kids grow—to spend the rest of our lives together.

"We'll even call him tonight so you can talk to him, okay?"

That seemed to perk Jacquie up a bit, and, of course, they had no trouble reaching me at my office at that time. "Now what will

I tell the kids when they want to talk to their dad?" she asked over the phone.

"You'll think of something," her mother consoled.

"Yep, I always do, don't I?"

Saudi Arabian Desert, February 1991:

The Army Blazer pulled into the Reserve Transportation Unit Transient Truck Stop about sixty kilometers north of Jubal. I emerged from the middle seat brushing away the desert dust and putting on my boonie hat while Lieutenant Colonel Jones, doing the same, looked up in time to return a salute rendered by a passing soldier.

Major Murray and Sergeant Major Helms were doing the same, while stretching their limbs. The transient point was set up along the main highway running along the Persian Gulf northwest to Khafji and then into Kuwait. The marines were somewhere in that vicinity; I thought maybe they were Safaniya.

The transient point was nothing more than a tent village. Some tents were set up as offices. A few of the tents had bunks for the weary traveler to take a load off and to catch some shut-eye. Like any five-star hotel, there was the entertainment area, comprised of a larger tent with rows of chairs and a large-screen TV, VCR, and a stack of VHS tapes.

The other end of the tent hosted a reading area with a makeshift library of paperback books. There was one tent that I desperately needed, the mess hall. I needed some grub and a hot cup of Joe.

Caffeine dependency was a universal plight of many soldiers. I found the mess hall and quickly appropriated a cup of coffee. Sugar and cream were not necessary. Mine was the color and consistency of Saudi crude oil.

The mess hall was a popular place. MREs (meals ready to eat) were the standard fare. There were also items that had arrived in care packages from the States. I dug around to look for something sweet and chocolaty.

Not a typical truck stop, numerous military cargo trucks and fuel tankers were parked in a disorderly manner across the greased-stained desert sand. The transient point not only filled up the soldiers but their vehicles as well. It was the military equivalent of a truck stop. Flocks of camels and shepherded by Bedouins marched across the horizon.

"This looks like paradise," the sergeant major said sarcastically.

First looking at his watch, Lieutenant Colonel Jones said, "Let's go in here and see if we can find something to eat. Major Gerblick won't be here for another hour."

The four of us sat around trying to stay busy, and after two hours without any sign of Major Gerblick, Lieutenant Colonel Jones walked over to me. "We're going to head back. You should be all right here. Just keep an eye out for him. He probably just got held up. He'll get here."

"No problem, sir," I answered. "I'll keep a lookout for him."

"All right, we'll catch you down the road later. Good luck," Lieutenant Colonel Jones told me as he shook my hand and then returned my salute. The commander turned around and headed back toward the Blazer with Major Murray and the sergeant major, both of whom also shook my hand and wished me the best.

I walked over to the movie tent and took a seat next to a disinterested soldier. The movie *Platoon* was on, so I got up and left.

Deciding to go for a walk, I canvassed the area and prayed, quoting the verse for the day in my journal—*Because you were slain, and with your blood you purchased men for God from every tribe and language and people and nation (Revelation 5:9-NLT).*

Time crawled like a slow-moving camel caravan trudging aimlessly along through the waves of sand. The hazy red sun sank below the surface of nowhere. Still nursing my cup of coffee, I stepped out of the tent and began to walk around the perimeter of the transient point.

The sky was turning black. There were no city lights, and the surrounding area was virtually blacked out so that the stars glowed like magic diamonds.

As I wandered about the perimeter my mind wandered as well. The desert is a very quiet place, and sounds can travel great distances. I closed my eyes for a moment and listened.

Sounds from the movie tent blared with the mixed clatter from the mess hall. Gentle snoring was coming from some of the barrack tents. Off in the distance I could hear the sound of the sheep and Bedouins.

All of these reverberations assailed my mind—those that represented life of human culture and religion. *Did any of these people know God?* We were in a war zone. Death has a way of happening in a war. After death, what next? The Bible said that every man had an appointment with death, and after that came judgment. This judgment would determine the final resting place of the dead—heaven or hell.

I suddenly noticed a major, cigar in one hand, emerge from a Humvee that was pulling into the area, kicking up sandy dust. He was looking around as if he was searching for someone. I walked toward him, trying not to be too conspicuous as I looked for his name tag.

The major saw me approaching. "Are you Lieutenant Meehan?" he asked.

"Yes, sir, that would be me. You must be Major Gerblick," I said after saluting him and reaching out to shake his hand.

"Yep. I'm glad to see you. Where's your stuff?"

"I have two duffels in the holding tent. I'll go grab them."

"I'll go with you. How long have you been waiting here?" Major Gerblick asked while looking over the hodgepodge of soldiers, vehicles, and tents.

"Not too long, sir, a couple of hours or so maybe," I answered, not wanting to let on that the four hours of waiting had seemed like an eternity.

Grabbing my bags, we threw them on the back of the Humvee and spun away, kicking up sand until we reached the hardtop and then headed north along the only major highway. Major Gerblick explained that the reason he was late was that he had to move out with the marines as they located to a new position.

Then Major Gerblick talked excitedly about the prospects of war, all while sweeping his cigar in animated circles in the night air with enthusiasm. I, on the other hand, was keeping a close eye on the large green signs that came into view as they were illuminated by the headlights:

Khafji 70 km
Kuwait City 170 km

As Major Gerblick continued to speak enthusiastically about the new technology of war, the orange glow of his cigar danced in the night like a firefly.

"You don't smoke, do ya, LT?"

"No, sir."

"Good, it's a bad habit. Anyway, as I was saying, this is the time for you to shine!" Major Gerblick continued with childlike glee. "This is great stuff. You can make a name for yourself in this conflict! Don't worry; everything will be fine. We got the best, most modern military hardware money can buy, and we're really doing a number on those guys with our bombardments and precision guided missiles! You know about those things, don't you LT?"

"Yes, sir, I watched them perform on TV while in Riyadh," I answered.

Khafji 30 km
Kuwait City 130 km

We had just passed another green sign as we continued toward the site where the Iraqis had tried their first ground offensive into Saudi Arabia but were held back by the United States Marines. Now I would soon join them for the remainder of the war.

Finally, before we reached Khafji, we turned off the main road and headed toward a group of flickering lights in the distance. *Thank God,* I thought. *We're not going into Kuwait tonight.* The rumbling of countless generators pierced the otherwise quiet night as we approached the marine compound.

"Here we are, LT—short for lieutenant. Get some sleep. We have a long day ahead of us tomorrow. We're moving out again, for the last time!"

I was already aware that the coalition ground forces were moving back and forth across the sandy roads in massive convoys as countless units jockeyed for their final position to launch the impending ground attack into Kuwait and Iraq. The road most traveled in these instances was known as *Tap Line Road*. I guessed that we would head a bit northwest and take up positions just south of the border, poised to strike the Kuwaiti airfields held by Saddam's army.

For now, I would pull out my sleeping bag and lay it on the canvassed cot stretched out for me in a small room with three others who were already sleeping. Stretching out on the hard army-issued cot, I stared at the dark ceiling above me and said a prayer for Trena, Aaron, and Jacquie. *Lord, I really want to see them again. Oh, how I miss them.*

Fayetteville, North Carolina

During the day, Trena was at the Eighth PSYOP Battalion helping other wives put together boxes for their husbands in the Middle East. All of the kids were present as well, since it was purposely planned for after-school hours. Each family member added his or her own special touch to the care packages, as well as slipping in letters and cards addressed directly to their loved one.

Later that night, as Trena put Aaron and Jacquie down for the night, she said, "Let's remember Daddy and all of those other dads tonight."

"Is Daddy in a safe place?" Jacquie asked.

"With God's protection, he's always in a safe place; but we can't forget to pray for him," Trena answered with firm belief in the power of prayer.

She could hear them whispering as she left them for the night, and was encouraged when she heard them giggling. Instead of telling them to get quiet and get some sleep, Trena welcomed their laughter of innocence. Intending to turn on CNN News for the latest, she laid down the controller and headed to bed herself.

"I love you, Scott, and we are all praying for you."

CHAPTER 10

KIBRIT ENEMY PRISONER
OF WAR (EPW) CAMP
SAUDI ARABIAN DESERT
MARCH 1991

The mass of war-torn Iraqi prisoners huddled together around several small campfires behind the wired fence. Approximately four thousand of them were holding army-issued green wool blankets over their shoulders as they tried desperately to stay dry and warm. Staring wide-eyed in fear, the whites of their eyes contrasted with the oil-smoked, gloomy, and darkened sky that turned day into night.

The unnatural darkness crept in, blotting out the sun, courtesy of one of the most hideous attacks on nature ever witnessed. When Saddam's forces realized that defeat was imminent, they marked their retreat by setting ablaze the Kuwaiti oil fields in a final act of defiance.

"I guess if he can't have them, nobody can," I overheard one of the Marine guards say. The guard was one of approximately sixty armed Marines along with a Military Police National Guard unit from Puerto Rico consisting of approximately one hundred soldiers from the Eighty-Ninth Military Police Brigade. We were vastly outnumbered by the prisoners.

One afternoon, the Iraqi prisoners came in a caravan of flatbed cattle trucks with attached flatbed trailers. They were packed together like sheep going to slaughter. The fourth largest army in the world, prior to Desert Storm, looked shattered. I was leaving the EPW camp for the night and heading back to the marine base camp.

"Stop here a minute," I instructed my driver, Staff Sergeant Helmitt. "I want to count them."

Staff Sergeant Helmitt pulled up to the first truck in line trying to get into Kibrit. Both of us began to count the bewildered, demoralized men.

"I count sixty," I said.

"Both in the truck and trailer?" Staff Sergeant Helmitt asked.

"Both."

'Yes, sir, that's about right."

"Drive down the road. Let's see how many trucks there are."

Staff Sergeant Helmitt drove slowly past the trucks leading into the EPW camp and down Tap Line Road heading northwest. I began counting again—this time the number of trucks pulling trailers.

"My God, there are sixty trucks, all with trailers, packed with at least the same amount. That means there are at least thirty-six hundred prisoners!"

"At least they're unarmed," Staff Sergeant Helmitt added.

I thought of the verse in Matthew 9—*Jesus had compassion on them, because they were harassed and helpless, like sheep without a shepherd.*

The coalition bombing against the Iraqi army, comprised mostly of B-52s, had certainly taken its toll. I remembered one morning as a thunderous roar erupted in the background. Major Gerblick smiled as the ground around us shook and said, "Ahh, the sounds of freedom." We all knew that the war was going much quicker than anyone had anticipated, and, at the current speed, we would be going home much sooner, too.

One of the verses from Psalm stated that, *A thousand may fall at your side, ten thousand at your right hand, but it will not come near you.* Feeling that this was quite literally the time to hold onto such words, I quoted it so that Major Gerblick could hear me.

"That's good, LT," Major Gerblick responded.

Precision bombing was used to knock out the Iraqi Military Command & Control and Communications. Infrastructure was replaced by massive continuous carpet bombing on the frontline

Iraqi soldiers. Tens of thousands surrendered but not before thousands died from this aerial US Air Force onslaught.

I rode back with Staff Sergeant Helmitt each morning after breakfast. We would participate in the interrogation process, which amounted to nothing more than questioning.

I was up close to the enemy once again, only this time they had been soundly defeated. I found myself actually feeling a bit sorry for them. I could see the helplessness in their eyes—eyes that belonged to the men of the "fourth largest army in the world," a fact that was mentioned over and over again while I was attending the Military Intelligence School at Fort Huachuca.

I could still here the instructors' words, "The Iraqis are hardened and experienced from recent fighting against the Iranians for nearly ten years. It's going to be bloody over there." The instructors felt that it was their duty to tell our class that "many of you sitting right here will go over there and never come back."

As more and more Iraqi soldiers were questioned, it became apparent that both soldiers and civilians alike were taken from their simplistic lives in places such as Baghdad, Kirkuk, and Mosul, and then thrown into the frontline trenches to face the coalition's air bombardment night and day. Completely subdued, they were ready to do or say anything that would appease the Americans who held them captive.

Islam had taught them to believe that their fate rested in Allah's hand, but for now their basic survival instincts told them it was someone else, the American warrior, who controlled their immediate destiny.

All of the prisoners seemed eager and willing to cooperate with us, and one of my objectives was to gain strategic information from them. A few secret police mixed in with the throngs were still spitting their poisonous threats at the prisoners. "Don't forget, we know where your family lives," they would threaten.

Many still believed in the "long arm of Saddam's law." The more timid prisoners still feared Saddam because, as they told us, "His men are everywhere." However, those from a Shi'a background were embolden by what they saw and heard, and, feeling safe in the hands of the Americans, were ready to give up Saddam's henchmen at the drop of a hat, or were devising a way to take care of them on their own.

I thought back to the first time I was ever involved in an interrogation. It was with an Iraqi defector who had escaped prior to the ground war. When I first saw him, I chuckled. The blindfold was lifted from his eyes. He looked like Bruce Springsteen; I hoped he'd sing. He hoped to eat. I thought about asking him where he'd left his guitar. The young Iraqi was obviously elated to be out of the trenches and allowed to eat food, which he devoured like a ravenous wolf.

I sat on a bench facing a wooden table with three chairs. A Reserve PSYOP captain from Minnesota conducted the interrogation. Facing him was the Saudi interpreter, Mohammed, and the prisoner, Bruce. He had been escorted by a marine guard and another marine staff sergeant. Both the prisoner and Mohammed had their backs to me.

The Iraqi had an oversized olive-drab field jacket on. His fatigues were tattered, his shoes had holes, and a dirty cotton T-shirt was used as a blindfold. One of the guards put on a pair of rubber gloves before removing it from the prisoner's head.

The marine staff sergeant sat down on the bench next to me behind the prisoner. After listening to the Iraqi talk and the Saudi interpret, the staff sergeant would disgustedly say to me in a whisper, "That's not what he said."

"So, you know Arabic?" I asked, a bit surprised.

"I'm from Lebanon," the staff sergeant replied.

My attention was back on the questioning now.

"Are you and your soldiers ready to fight us?" the Reserve PSYOP officer asked.

"Nobody wants to fight you Americans. We want to surrender," the Iraqi said through an interpreter.

"How many want to surrender?"

"All of us. We are very tired and hungry. Nobody wants to fight."

"Then why don't more of you come over to us and surrender like you?"

"They can't. They will be shot. Our families are threatened," he said dejectedly.

"They didn't shoot you. Why did you come?"

"I was sent on an errand, and I just kept walking into the night desert. They couldn't see me, but I heard them yell. I ran fast! I couldn't take it anymore."

The PSYOP Reserve captain from Minnesota looked up at me briefly and then continued his questioning.

"How is everybody's morale in your unit?"

The Saudi interpreter tried to explain the meaning of what he was just asked.

"It's very bad. Nobody wants to fight. Everybody is hungry."

"They don't feed you?"

"With what? There isn't any more food. Our supplies have been cut off. If somebody dies, we split his rations."

It appeared that the captain was finished asking him questions when the prisoner held out a crumpled piece of paper and showed it to him. The captain held it up for me to see.

"That's one of our leaflets," I told him. "It explains that they will be fed if they come over to us."

The Iraqi started to turn his head behind him to see who was talking from behind. The Lebanese staff sergeant shouted something at him in Arabic, and he quickly looked straight ahead at the captain.

I stood up and nodded to the captain and told him that was one of our products. Looking back at the prisoner, "Did you see a lot of these?" the captain asked, knowing that planeloads were dropped over the front lines.

"Yes, of course. They're everywhere. We all have them. We grab them when no one is watching."

"Do you and the other soldiers believe them?" he asked.

"Yes. Everything you show us is true. We don't believe Saddam anymore. When will you attack us? If you attack us now, everybody will surrender. Believe me!" The Iraqis voice was pleading.

I glanced at the captain, nodded my head in appreciation, and went back to sit down on the bench. After a few more questions, the marine guard walked over and put the ragged-looking blindfold back over the Iraqi's eyes. The staff sergeant got up and followed them down the wooden corridor. That was the end.

I returned to our camp and reported what had taken place to Major Gerblick. I also told him that the marines had interrogated the prisoners for tactical information and then were sending them away to other camps. We were lucky to nab "Bruce Springsteen."

Major Gerblick brought this to the attention of a staff officer of General Boomer, who then arranged for any English-speaking or high-ranking prisoners to be sent to our PSYOP group. General Boomer's intent was to gain a psychological and strategic perspective from the enemy on the lines and their state of mind.

One such Iraqi prisoner interrogation by our PSYOP team went something like this:

"So, you know English. Where did you learn it?" the Iraqi was asked.

"I'm an American," he answered. "I'm from Michigan."

Everybody laughed. "No way. How did you get here like this if you're an American?"

Speaking like an American, the Iraqi replied, "It's true, you just gotta believe me. I was in Baghdad visiting my cousins, and we decided to go to a local disco. Next thing you know, a bunch of Saddam's troops barge in with their weapons and haul all the males out of the place and into trucks. Then, there I was, held at gunpoint in a truck and being driven to the front lines. Please! Please! I beg you; take me home!"

After a typical day at the EPW camp, Staff Sergeant Helmitt and I would drive back to the camp of tents surrounded by sand berms (man-made hills from sand). We arrived at our dimly lit PSYOP HQ tent and joined Major Gerblick, Major Tristchler, the S-3, and 1SG Steinberg, who ran the logistics for the team and babysat the major's driver, PFC Hathaway. Every evening, we would all sit around the field table and just shoot the breeze.

I walked over to the care box and pulled out two packages of instant oatmeal. "Ummm, there's still some brown sugar and cinnamon," I said with satisfaction.

"So, sit down and tell me about your day, LT," Major Gerblick said with interest.

I relayed the events of the day at the office and divulged any pertinent intelligence he might find useful.

Most of our talk, however, switched gears drastically from the battle situation to our soon upcoming journey home, which would begin within days—far quicker than anyone had ever anticipated.

It had only been fourteen days before that I had stood with hundreds of marines surrounding a makeshift wooden platform. Standing on the platform with his hands on his hips, Lieutenant General Boomer declared, "Next Stop—Kuwait!" Marines raised their fists and yelled out in victorious cheers.

In only two more days, our team would be joining the I-MEF in a convoy of fighting men and return to the port of Jubal. There, we would begin our closing operation procedures and awards, and then the trip home. From Jubal, the PSYOP team would return to Riyadh and then proceed through the exiting from Riyadh for the journey home.

When the chitchat ended each evening, usually late, I sometimes walked out to one of the sand berms and looked out into the darkness.

Not long before the ground war kicked off, I would often go outside under the stars before going to bed and watch the lights in the sky moving north and south as if they were cars on an interstate highway. These were the coalition aircraft flying toward their targets on nonstop sorties. Way over the horizon, the pitched black sky was met with a bright orange hue rising from the ground after one of the airstrikes.

On my last night there in the desert, I walked over to another berm facing north. It seemed like an ideal time to give God a word of thanks and to come up with another appropriate verse. Digging into my cargo pocket and pulling out my pen light and small Bible, I found the words, "Where the storm has swept by, the wicked are gone, but the righteous stand firm forever" (Proverbs 10:25).

Riyadh, Saudi Arabia

Just like that, the first Gulf War was over. I left the vast sands of the northern Saudi desert and traveled with the marines to Jubal on the Persian Gulf coast. I didn't stay long before moving on to Riyadh to link up with the main body of my unit. *I'll get to stay in Eskan Village again*, I thought somewhat pleasantly, knowing that it was the last stop before heading back home, my ultimate goal.

Residing in the same villa and room from which I had left, I was glad to learn that there was no longer any night shift to pull. I was also elated to find several packages, boxes, and letters waiting for me from Trena, the kids, and many others. Aaron and Jacquie both had really enjoyed the postcards I had sent them from the desert.

Cutting out the front cover of an MRE box, I had written on the unmarked inside and had even drawn a picture of a camel for each of them. The front side of the homemade postcard was labeled Chocolate Chip Cake along with the trademark.

As things continued to wind down, I learned that Lieutenant Colonel Jones wanted to talk to me. I reported to him immediately.

"Lieutenant Meehan, please sit down."

"Yes, sir!"

"You did a great job out there, according to Major Gerblick, and we really appreciate your efforts."

"Thank you, sir."

"I have an important mission for you to carry out. I need you to fly back to Bragg in the C-141 with all of our equipment. I'll assign you three NCOs, but you'll be in charge of seeing that everything gets back home."

"Yes, sir."

"It will be the day after we arrive with the main body, and you'll arrive around 0300 without any fanfare."

"Yes, sir."

"Any questions?"

"No, sir."

"Good. We'll send you down to Dhahran with some NCOs in a deuce early next week. You'll load the pallets with all of the equipment to take back home. A C-141 will be there ready to receive the pallets."

"Okay, sir," I said, standing up, following the commander's cue. After rendering a smart salute, I was out the door, trying not to show my disappointment.

That's just great, I thought to myself. *Everybody else gets to fly on a commercial 747, land at Pope AFB in the afternoon to throngs of family members and a band, and I get stuck in a cargo jet with an ETA of 0300.*

I had to maintain my hard stance and reputation, one that was pinned on me for coming back from the front lines unscathed. Besides, I reasoned with myself, the power of prayer always works. So, I began praying as soon as I was given the mission that something would work out where I, too, could be on that 747 and receive a warm welcome home by my wife and kids like everybody else.

The HQ Company commander, Captain Nelson, and I began doing things together, working out at the gym and finding rides downtown a couple of times before the day of departure to take advantage of the gold markets. There, I bartered for some nice silver and gold pieces. Jacquie would get a silver camel necklace, and Trena would receive a necklace with nine golden hearts, the number of years we had been married.

That was a no-brainer purchase once I spotted it among the throngs of dazzling gold pieces. Aaron would get a puzzle ring. I felt sorry for the Saudi women who stopped and watched us along with other Americans. These Saudi women often paid the price of being chased away with clubs by the religious police.

The day of departure came, with four NCOs and me leaving for Dhahran in two cargo trucks and a Humvee. Once we arrived at the airfield, and after checking in with the air force manifest office, I began hastily to unload the equipment from the trucks onto the pallets.

The big Pan Am 747 loomed large in the background farther down the tarmac. I was praying fervently for a miracle switch to take place even though Trena was just very happy to have me home no matter how and when I arrived.

In the next several hours we were able to load everything onto two pallets. Afterward, tired from our efforts, we went to get some dinner at the DFAC on the airbase. Dismissing the soldiers for the evening, I told my driver to head back to the staging area so I could report to Lieutenant Colonel Jones, who had just arrived with two busloads of soldiers from Riyadh moments before.

My Humvee pulled up just as the PSYOP Group personnel were unloading and beginning the process of leaving the country through military customs. Finding Lieutenant Colonel Jones first, I reported on the cargo status, received a "good job" response, and then began walking around the area, trying not to look too discouraged.

Just then, Staff Sergeant Pendergrass, the operations NCO, approached me as I was talking through the fence to Captain Nelson. Staff Sergeant Pendergrass and I had worked together on the night shift before I had left for the duty with the marines in the desert.

"Hey, sir, you wanna get on this flight?"

Trying to contain my enthusiasm, I nonetheless exclaimed, "Sure do. How?"

"Well, don't say anything yet, but the ol' man is mad that everyone is here except Captain Badley, who's somewhere downtown schmoozing with the Saudis. He told me if Badley doesn't show in five minutes, he's switching him with you. Where's your stuff; is it with you?"

"No," I said with my heart sinking, "but I can get it in twenty minutes."

"All right. Hurry! I won't say anything."

As I instructed the driver to break speeding records on the way back to the Khobar Towers where I had left all my gear, Captain Badley was dropped off by some friends and told to report to Lieutenant Colonel Jones. When I arrived back at the airbase with my gear, I saw Staff Sergeant Pendergrass and asked, "Am I too late?"

"No, get your stuff and go through the line."

Words could not describe my feelings. "Oh, wow, man, thank you so much. I owe you big."

"You can buy me a beer back home," he answered.

"Hey, could you get a message to my wife about me being with the main body?"

"Sure, sir, give me your number."

I quickly jotted it down, thanked him again profusely, processed through the air force immigration setup, and gladly waited for boarding.

The flight was full of uniformed officers and soldiers, all from a variety of units other than ours. Everyone was in a jubilant mood, except, I would imagine, Badley, who I had replaced.

As the sun began to rise, it was evident that loads of the boxed goods that had been sent from the United States to all the soldiers were stacked on pallets all over the tarmac. But the war was over so quickly that most everybody was either home or in the process of leaving for home. I often wondered what happened to all of those goodies sent from home.

The wheels left the land of Arabia, and I hoped that I would never see that place again. We stopped in Rome, Italy, for refueling and then landed in Bangor, Maine, where a couple in their seventies came aboard and passed out miniature American flags, all the while thanking the soldiers for what they had accomplished. Then we were airborne once again with one more stop at JFK in New York City.

Soon enough, the Pan Am jet began its final approach over Spring Lake, North Carolina, and Fort Bragg as it landed on the tarmac at Pope Air Force Base. As soon as the wheels touched, the whole plane erupted with loud cheering, yelling, and clapping.

After the plane taxied for what seemed like hours, we waited and waited. Apparently it was taking some time and effort to coordinate everything on the ground. The efforts of getting the band set up and other logistics had been complicated by a thunderstorm that had just passed over Pope Air Force Base.

When I crossed the doorframe onto the top platform of the silver, gliding stairs, I stopped briefly and looked toward the bleachers, which were full of people cheering. Someone next to me said, "There's someone here for Scott Meehan." I looked and saw that there was a large, orange, florescent sign with big black letters: "Welcome Home, Scott Meehan!"

I smiled and proudly said, "That's my wife!"

After several more minutes of lining up in the correct formation, our large returning group marched forward to the beat of a drum and stopped long enough to listen to a welcome home speech. We were released to our loved ones . . . momentarily. We would still have to check in our weapons at the unit before being released for the day to go home.

I walked immediately toward the pretty brunette holding the flashy glowing sign up high toward the sky, all the while bumping into and getting bumped by throngs of people in the process. It was a good thing she stood her ground with the sign. She had chosen the florescent orange sign because she was planning on me arriving at three in the morning.

Before Trena spotted me, Aaron and Jacquie ran up to me yelling, "Daaaady!"

Bending down to give them a warm embrace without conking them on the head with the butt of my rifle, I was full of laughter and joy to see my kids again. Then before I could fully come to a straight stand, Trena nearly knocked me over as she ran into me with wide-open arms, accompanied with tears of joy and a smattering of kisses, which I happily returned.

I discovered that the whole event was captured on a home video camera. Trena had her best friend, Karen, in control of recording the historic moment.

After our weapons were turned into the arms room, I was able to finally go home and be with my family once again. "Well, everybody, our prayers were answered, right?" I stated.

"Yep!" both kids answered as if it couldn't have been any other way.

CHAPTER 11

DEFENSE ACQUISITIONS
ORLANDO, FLORIDA
1998-2002

I walked along the sidewalk circling the building in the middle of the night, desperately pleading with God that I would be allowed to stay in Orlando and not have to move again. The walking and pleading had become a nightly vigil, and it was accompanied with a fasting of various degrees. *Lord, I'm sure this is where you want me to be, but I need a miracle if I'm going to stay.*

Three years before, in July 1997, I had begun my company-level command. This meant that I was in complete charge of approximately one hundred soldiers, and was responsible for their every action and duty. My command was at Macgregor Range, about thirty miles north of El Paso and Fort Bliss, Texas. The range contained 1.4 million acres of land, as it was designed for the Patriot Missile firings from the air defense units located at Fort Bliss.

Just before taking the reins from my predecessor, I was notified by the army that I was no longer in the military intelligence branch but had been accepted into the acquisition branch. Not understanding the full implication, I called to find out some facts. My call reached a Major Merth.

"I understand that I have been accepted into the Acquisition Corps," I began.

"Yes, congratulations!"

"Could you tell me what all of this means for the road ahead?"

"I'd be glad to," she responded. "First, you need to have a command." (A command is when an officer is placed in charge of a unit of soldiers.)

I quickly interjected. "I'm in a command position now."

"Great! You are ahead of the game! After you have finished your command, we want to send you to the advanced civil schooling program so that you can obtain your master's degree."

"Awesome!" I replied. "Where will I go to school?"

"You tell us where you want to go, and then we'll need to approve it. However, you will need to study something in the computer sciences. How does this all sound to you?"

I couldn't believe my ears. "Great! When do you need to know what school?"

"As soon as possible."

"Okay, I'll get back with you by the end of the week. Will that be good?"

"That's fine, and congratulations once again!"

"Thank you very much!" I replied, quite gratefully.

As expected, Trena was thrilled with the news!

"Where shall I tell her we want to go?" I asked Trena.

"Tell her you want someplace in Florida!" Trena said with a chuckle.

"I can do that!"

"Let me think on that one. When does she need to know?" she added.

"We have a couple of days."

My command would last for a total of twelve to fifteen months, which was usually the case. We had some time. By the end of the week, Trena had confided that although she really wanted to go to Florida, she wanted me to first ask the new branch manager where my next assignment was going to be. That way, she wisely deduced, the kids won't have to keep changing schools.

"Let's pray about it," I said, knowing that she already had been praying, just as was I.

I called Major Merth before the end of the week.

"Well, have you decided where you want to go?" she began.

"Can I ask where you intend to assign me and then choose based on that? That way, there will be a lot less traveling involved, and I can save the government some money," I quickly added.

"Ahh, okay, that's a good idea. How would you like to go to Florida?" she asked.

I could hardly contain my excitement. Keeping my composure, I replied, "Great, what units are there?"

"We could send you to STRICOM (Simulations Training and Instrumentation Command) in Orlando or CENTCOM (Central Command) in Tampa."

"Either would be fine by me!" I exclaimed.

"Okay, let's do this. Get accepted into one of the colleges or universities in those areas that have a computer program, and then we'll take it from there."

After writing several institutions—UCF, USF, University of Tampa, Webster University—I moved forward with Webster University, located in Orlando. It was the fastest institution to respond with all the necessary transitional paperwork. I was accepted into their program and would pursue a degree in computer resource information management.

During my command, it became my regular practice to take my lunch to OP 5 (observation point) where the Patriot missile firings could be observed, and just sit on the bleachers. Here, I reflected on the past duty and wondered about the path to the future. Praying and reading the Bible was part of my lunch routine.

"I am sending an angel ahead of you to guard you along the way and to bring you to the place I have prepared" (Exodus 23:20). This is what I read while sitting at OP 5 at Macgregor Range when I requested favor in finding a new home, neighborhood, church, school for the kids, and job for me and Trena. I felt the same peace that I'd had after walking away from the phone booth in San Antonio back in '81.

I thought of the time when one of my soldiers, Sergeant First Class Kuntz, came to me and told me about the conversation he'd had with another sergeant first class, Linden. Both were well-respected leaders of soldiers assigned under my responsibility.

"What do you think of our new commander?" Linden had asked while shooting billiards.

"He's all right; I like him," Kuntz answered. "Why?"

"I don't know; I can't put my finger on it, but he's different," Linden stated.

"How so?" asked Kuntz.

"Well, he never curses, doesn't seem to get angry, and doesn't talk like the other commanders we've had."

"He's religious," Kuntz answered.

"I don't know; they all say that. Yeah, maybe so, but he just seems to wear his religion on his sleeve or something."

Kuntz related this story to me and revealed Linden's assessment as if I should be made aware of it. I thought that his perspective was interesting but did nothing to alter my style of command.

A few months after Kuntz shared this story with me, he came up to me after formation one morning and said, "Sir, be praying. I invited SFC Linden to church with me on Sunday."

"I certainly will, Sergeant Kuntz. I think that's great."

On Monday, after the morning formation, Kuntz came running up to me excitedly.

"Sir, sir, he did it!" he exclaimed.

"Huh, did what, Sergeant Kuntz?"

"Sergeant Linden came to church with me in the morning, went forward to get saved, and came back that night to get baptized!" Kuntz said, smiling from ear to ear.

I smiled with him. "That's awesome, Sergeant Kuntz! Praise the Lord!"

If Linden's life changed because he had been observing my lifestyle, then my time as a battery commander was a complete success!

Everything that I had prayed about on OP 5 unfolded in Orlando. We found the house we were looking for with four bedrooms and a pool, in a great neighborhood; the church, pastored by a godly man with sound biblical principles; and the right school for the kids. The fifteen months that I attended Webster University went by quickly, and the program was a great success. I received my master's degree as a result.

After the degree program was completed, I was prepared to become a part of Simulations Training and Instrumentation Command (STRICOM). During this time of transition, however, the acquisition branch manager changed from Major Merth to a different person.

Upon graduation, I learned that he wanted to send me to Fort Gordon, Georgia, instead of keeping me in Orlando. This news came after we had bought a house, Trena had found a job, and the kids were settled in a good Christian school.

Obviously we were all quite disappointed. I was prepared to accept the outcome, with the plan of moving to Georgia by myself initially, and with plans for the family to join me later. Then, I felt the Holy Spirit prompt me to go on a prayer vigil that would include fasting certain things, something new each week, such as coffee one week, TV the next, etc.

This went on night after night, and week after week, until it was time for me to report to Fort Gordon. My reporting date was to be on the first of June 2000. Less than a week before leaving, I arrived home from church to find Trena waiting for me.

"A general called here looking for you. He wants you to call him back as soon as you get in no matter what time it is," Trena said as I came into the room.

"Really, was it General Bond?" I asked, knowing that he was the STRICOM commander.

"Yes, that's who it was."

I picked up the phone and dialed immediately.

"Hello?"

"General Bond, this is Captain Meehan. You wanted me to call you?"

"Yes, I understand that you want to work here for me."

"Yes, sir! That would be great!"

"Okay, don't pack your bags quite yet. I'll see what I can do. Give me a call tomorrow about the same time."

"Yes, sir, I will. Thank you!"

Trena was on the bed pumping her fist. "*Yeeesss!*"

The following night, the last one before the Memorial Day weekend, and the weekend I was scheduled to travel Fort Gordon, I called General Bond back . . . right after one last prayer.

"Hello?"

"Sir, this is Captain Meehan again, just checking on my status."

"You're not going anywhere but here! I got you!" He said firmly.

"Thank you so much, sir!"

"Don't mention it. I'll see you Tuesday."

To say that Trena and I were elated with this news would be an understatement.

My career was sailing along, and I felt good about my future prospects for promotion to the rank of major in the United States Army. While I was working toward my master's degree during the evenings at Webster University, I spent my days teaching basic computer to sixth-, seventh-, and eighth-graders at Faith Christian Academy, where Trena taught and Aaron and Jacquie attended.

All in all, everything was looking bright. We settled into our new luxurious (by military base housing standards) home and modest neighborhood in Orlando, Florida.

Then, the unexpected happened, which shocked both Trena and me to the core. The new promotion list to major was released shortly after I graduated from the advanced civil schooling (army terms while they paid for my education), and my name was not on it.

"There must be some mistake!" I exclaimed when first hearing the news by phone from my commanding officer, Brigadier General Bond. There was no mistake. The army didn't make these kinds of mistakes.

When I hung up and looked over at Trena, her mouth dropped open like a Floridian sinkhole and just hung, trying to find the words. I had no explanation, although Trena did offer comfort the best way she knew how to a deflated soldier's ego.

"What are we supposed to do now?" she asked.

"Well, although the odds are against it, I do receive a second look next year," I tried to reason hopefully. "The fact is, I may need to seriously start thinking about retirement if I can make it."

I quietly calculated in my head how many years I already had behind me, including my seven years of enlisted service.

"I would have thought that they would have kept you after sending you to get your master's degree," Trena added.

"I thought so too," I answered, still wondering what could possibly have gone wrong. All of my evaluations were good, and I was confused.

For the next several months, I gave it my all to try and become one of the best acquisition officers at STRICOM, now called PEO STRI. Although, I was learning on my feet without any formal education in acquisition management, I wasn't grasping my duty the way I felt I should be in order to manage a Constructive Simulation Program. I did not possess the knowledge of a software engineer that was necessary to comprehend the full scope of the program.

I immersed myself with many other volunteer projects such as Junior Achievement and various church activities. I had the gut feeling that my military talents were not maximized, and what was worse, I was not in any position to change my situation.

While I looked for ways to improve myself in the acquisition world and took on other projects different than constructive simulations, I was starting to enjoy the new responsibility of working with the Combat Training Centers and helping them with their needs with future combat systems.

One evening as I was on a flight to Washington, DC. to attend a meeting about the project, I began working on, ONESAF, a constructive simulation program. It was a model that was projected to consolidate all the military forces into a tracking system that could be monitored by future commanders and operation officers during training exercises and battle situations. I would chair the meeting logistically but allow the civilian SES officers to run the show.

Earlier that morning, while still at home and then later while Trena drove me to Orlando International Airport, I felt uneasy and decided at the last minute to put away my breakfast and fast with prayer instead. I really wasn't sure why I felt troubled, but knew in my heart that something just didn't seem right.

As the plane headed northeast from Orlando, I noticed a blanket of clouds stretched as far as I could see to the west. Another thin layer was above a small gap of blue sky in between the layers of clouds.

As the sun was beginning to descend and was positioned between the layers, the sun turned into a bright red ball that cast a red blanket effect onto the lower layer of clouds. The white-gray layer was turned into a violet blanket. The upper layer of clouds reflected a pinkish hue, and the clear patch of sky between the layers of clouds was now a solid dark crimson color.

Overwhelmed by God's awesome display of splendor, I immediately thought of the verse in Exodus when God was passing over the Israelites, "The blood will be a sign for you on the houses where you are; and when I see the blood, I will pass over you. No destructive plague will touch you when I strike" (Exodus 12:13). *If only America would claim the blood.*

Later that evening as the US Airway jet made its final approach into Reagan National, I felt the urgent need to pray earnestly throughout the landing. The passenger next to me, a Washingtonian, and I were watching the buildings along the Potomac River zoom past us as the plane was about to touch down.

Suddenly, the jet engines roared with a fury as if awakened from a slumber, and the front of the aircraft shifted upward in a defined attempt to take off from the tarmac.

The lady next to me turned to me looking horrified. "That's never happened before!"

Soon, the pilot's voice could be heard over the intercom.

"I apologize, ladies and gentlemen; it would seem that our friends on the ground had decided not to take off when they were supposed to, and we will just make a routine circle around the city and be on the ground shortly."

I was relieved that we were still talking and now fully airborne, streaking over the city of Washington. "Thank you, Lord," I whispered to myself.

The aircraft made a wide circle over the glittering city below as we began a second approach to the runway. I continued my prayer all the way through to touchdown. I was a little uneasy to see a line of emergency vehicles waiting along the side of the tarmac with their lights flashing.

When it was time to filter out of the aircraft, I passed the door to the cockpit and saw the pilot sitting in a chair, full of sweat and facing the exiting passengers.

"Everything all right?" I asked with a wry smile.

"Oh, sure, just routine," the pilot answered unconvincingly, sweat dripping down his brighter than normal, pale face.

Nearly a year later, the day came after a busy summer that I was supposed to find out whether the army would pick me up for major. I had a second chance. Otherwise, I was prepared to hear the dreaded words, "You weren't on the list."

My new commanding officer, Brigadier General Seay, had replaced BG Bond, and he would be the one to call me this time if I had not made the list. I wasn't sure that I was ready to be passed over for a second time. Could my ego take it? I was deflated by the first rejection and felt ashamed.

Although I felt apprehensive and felt a tinge of defeat, my spirits were still positive, mostly because of what had transpired over the past month. My son, Aaron, had graduated from high school and was accepted into West Point! That indeed was a family highlight for all to celebrate.

The four of us had driven to New York and involved ourselves with the Reception Day festivities, the period of time when the new recruits, recent high school graduates or graduates, began their life at the academy. Out of nearly six thousand candidates who applied from around the country during the past year, only twelve hundred were accepted. Now, they were going to get a first-hand taste of what they were really made of.

Though quite proud of Aaron, it was hard leaving the campus for our journey back south. It was especially hard for Trena. She was consoled only by the fact that we would go up to see him again a month later for Acceptance Day, when the cadets were accepted to continue after a grueling summer of military orientation.

While waiting to find out if I had made major on the second look against the odds, I kept busy with traveling to the Florida Keys with a group of youth from my church. We took them on a deep sea fishing expedition and to do some snorkeling. I also busied myself with a variety of other volunteer activities.

One of these was being the assigned casualty assistance officer for a widow, Ursula Nazario, from Berlin, who was married to an American soldier that had recently passed away. She witnessed the Russian soldiers enter her city toward the end of World War II.

When the assignment was complete, I kept in touch with her, and for the next several years Ursula and I would meet, along with Trena, and have lunch together about once a month, a practice that continues to this day.

Then the phone call came. Would this be the end of my twenty-one-year military career? The army had only given me credit for eighteen years because of the break in service. Still, it was enough, I thought, that if I was not picked up for major, the army would have to retain me until I was able to retire.

"Captain Meehan?" Brigadier General Seay asked.

"Yes, sir, this is Captain Meehan."

"I'm afraid it's not good news. You weren't picked up. They even stipulated that you had seven months to depart from the army."

"But, sir," I interjected. "I have more than eighteen years of service, and I believe they have to retain me until I retire."

"You do?" Brigadier General Seay sounded surprised. "Yes, of course they do. Come by the office tomorrow, and we'll contact branch to verify," Seay said, sounding a bit more cheerful himself after delivering bad news.

"All right, sir, I'll be there," I answered, believing that I would at least be able to retire as a captain.

Sure enough, we discovered that the US Army would indeed retain me until I reached my twenty-year mark and be able to retire. Both Trena and I were relieved to hear that news.

When I was an enlisted medic stationed in Berlin I remember how some of the soldiers had told me that they were being processed out of the army just prior to when they would reach eligibility to retire. "That's not right," I would tell them. But it was a fact, at least in the eighties.

Although it appeared to be the end of the road for me as a military officer, I plowed ahead with vigor, determined to show anybody and everybody who may have been watching, even if it was only God, that a mistake had been made in letting me out of the service.

Orlando, Florida to Seattle, Washington September 10, 2001

I was on my way to Fort Lewis, Washington, to conduct meetings with some of the commanders and operations officers about the newly fielded Stryker vehicles. The vehicles were scheduled to make their way to Fort Polk and take part in high-profile exercises.

It was one of my responsibilities to ensure that the new instrumentation system being installed at the JRTC would be sufficient to communicate with the Stryker vehicles conducting their exercises.

The vehicles were to be fitted with the EPLARS (Enhanced Precision Locating and Reporting System) and the FBCB2 (Force XXI Battle Command, Brigade-and-Below) which provided situational awareness, and command and control to the lowest tactical echelons, or quite simply, the troops who were on the ground.

I also had to ensure a seamless facilitation between the flow of battle on the ground to interoperate with the main instrumentation systems at the JRTC and to ensure that there was sufficient funding for the project.

I was looking forward to the trip for two reasons. First, I had never been to the Pacific Northwest. Second, I recently had discovered that one of my SF buddies, Mike Yorgensen, had just retired from the army and was working at the army hospital there. Reminiscing about the early training days would be fun.

My flight was long and uneventful, but I remembered how spectacular Mount Rainer looked in the clear blue sky as I watched it pass on the left side of the aircraft. I even remembered telling a fellow passenger who was afraid to fly that she had nothing to worry about and that all would be safe.

Portland, Maine September 11, 2001

Two men, Mohamed Atta and another, Al-Omari, checked out of the Comfort Inn and left for the Portland International Jetport (Matthews 2006). Their plane left at 6:00 a.m. for Logan International Airport in Boston. They sat together in the very back of the plane. Because of the terminal's arrangement in Boston, they would not be required to go through a security check again.

Their trip was uneventful, and before long, the two boarded American Airlines Flight 11 to San Francisco (Matthews 2006). Atta was checked in under the name Mohamed Atta and was seated back in the eighth row. At 7:59 a.m., the plane departed from Boston, carrying eighty-one passengers.

At 8:28 a.m., the plane's transponder was turned off, and Atta announced over the intercom, "We have control of the plane. Just stay quiet and everything will be okay. If you try to make any moves you'll endanger yourself and the airplane. Just stay quiet." Seconds later, the American Airlines jetliner crashed into the north tower of the World Trade Center.

Fort Lewis, Washington September 11, 2001

I was just waking after a fitful night of sleep. After rolling over to answer my wakeup call, I slowly got up and read the instructions to the particular coffee pot placed in my room and the packaged coffee to match. Once I had that running, I headed for the shower.

Going through my routine, futile attempts to make myself look younger and better, I headed back out to my room and switched on the news. Glancing at my watch, I saw that it was about a quarter to six in the morning. I wanted a good breakfast and a robust start to the day consisting of long meetings and a possible visit with Yorgi.

The news events on the television suddenly caught my attention. While watching black billows of smoke rushing from one of the World Trade Center towers as the newscasters tried to guess what had happened, another jet appeared on the screen from nowhere and crashed into the second tower.

"My God, what is happening?" I exclaimed aloud. I headed to the phone to call Trena after watching the events unfold on the screen before my eyes. She would be at school this time of the morning, I reasoned, so I called the school office.

"Hello?" Trena answered.

"Are you seeing this stuff on the news?" I asked frantically.

"Yes, we're watching right now."

"They just hit the Pentagon!" I exclaimed as another news bulletin appeared on the screen. Listen, I doubt that these meetings will take place here this week, so I'll try to get home as soon as I can."

"All right, but I believe that they are grounding all flights for now," Trena replied.

"Great," I said. "Maybe I can come home by train or something. I'll call you later."

It took me nearly two hours to get through the front gate into Fort Lewis from where I was staying just outside the premises.

As predicted, most all of the army forces stationed at Fort Lewis were busy with real life missions, as they are called, and caught up with the latest threat to our national security. All scheduled meetings were put on hold indefinitely.

I took advantage of my time there, after finding out that the earliest I could leave would be the fifteenth. I visited the army hospital and surprised Mike Yorgensen with a nice, short visit.

Years earlier, Mike had decided to attend the physician assistant course and ended up becoming an army PA after serving many years with the Special Forces as an enlisted soldier. I had not seen him since the early eighties at Fort Bragg. We figured that it had been nineteen years!

Recently retired, he maintained the same job, family practice, as he did when he was active duty. Even his office stayed the same. The only thing different about Mike was that his thin, balding hair was much longer.

"It's great seeing you again after all these years," I began.

"It has been a long time, hasn't it? How's Trena?"

"She's doing well, thanks. I told her that I would try to see you while out here."

"Tell her hi for me. So, what are you up to? I heard that you were involved in something in Berlin."

"Huh? Who told you that?" I truly wondered.

"Oh, we have ears. Word gets around," Yorgi said.

"You tell me. What did you hear?"

Yorgi laughed. "Don't worry about it. Tell me what you've been up to."

We caught each other up on old times and discussed the events that had transpired that rocked the world. Neither of us volunteered to be the Monday morning quarterback and explain our own theory for the reason something like that could ever have taken place.

Both of us knew, however, that things would be different in our world. The Cold War was over but a new kind of war had just begun.

Five months later, a very unusual thing happened on the night of February 21, 2002. I dreamt that my commanding officer, Brigadier General Seay, was telling me to get my promotion board packet ready for a third look.

"But, sir," I remembered vividly from my dream, "you have the wrong person. I was passed over twice and am retiring, remember?"

"Get it done, Captain Meehan!" Those were his firm, fading words as I woke up in the middle of the night wondering if I should wake up Trena and share this dream with her. I decided to wait until morning. I usually don't remember my dreams and hoped that I wouldn't forget this one in the morning.

Later that day, still bothered by that dream, I called my new branch manager, not the one in 2000; in Washington and asked if it was possible for me to submit another packet to the promotion board since I had already been passed over twice. His answer surprised me. "Well, since you are still in the army, nobody can really stop you. Go for it."

I went home to discuss this new bit of information with Trena, and after determining that there certainly wasn't anything to lose, I put together a packet suitable for the promotion board that included a fresh photo and pertinent information concerning my latest achievements as an assistant product manager with the Stryker vehicle connectivity into the JRTC.

Seven months later, my new boss, Lieutenant Colonel Mullins, walked into my office cubicle followed by Colonel Reyenga.

"Congratulations, Major Meehan!" said Lieutenant Colonel Mullins as he handed me some major rank pins. I was speechless! This promotion was nothing short of a miracle! Both Trena and I knew this to be true. Nobody else had ever heard of such a thing. Promoted on the third look!

Before I knew it, I was slotted for an assignment to Riyadh, Saudi Arabia. My function was going to change from program management to contracting, and I was to be the deputy directorate of contracting at Eskan Village, a place where I had spent time before during Desert Storm.

Two months prior to my scheduled departure from home for a full year, the US forces invaded Iraq.

After the Commissioning ceremony in Lakeland, Florida, with Trena's
mother and father (1989)

A dining-in during the Military Intelligence Officer Basic Course
at Fort Huachuca, Arizona (1990)

Our Psychological Operations team in a remote desert location during Desert Storm (1991)

Back home at Fort Bragg, North Carolina (1991)

Chapter 12

Déjà Vu
Riyadh, Saudi Arabia
June-September 2003

In my twenty-third year as an army veteran, I felt for sure that my gung ho days were over. I had a desk job in Riyadh, Saudi Arabia, that was supposed to last a full year. But the war in Iraq was in full swing and I soon received transfer orders reassigning me to Balad, Iraq; LSA Anaconda.

I would serve as a contingency contracting officer supporting more than twenty thousand soldiers, marines, and airmen as well as government civilians and contractors.

Two months before Saddam's capture, I was far removed from the action while performing my duties in Riyadh, Saudi Arabia. My title while in Riyadh was deputy directorate of contracting even though I had no contracting experience. This was one of those learn as you go jobs.

I was back at Eskan Village, but the atmosphere was much different than it was when I was there in 1991 during Desert Storm. There was only a fraction of the number of soldiers milling about, and everyone knew everybody else, much like the small mission base community where I lived in Colombia during high school. My living quarters was a six-bedroom villa, which I thankfully had to myself. During the war in 1991, when I was a second lieutenant, I shared the exact same type of villa with seven other officers.

Each evening, despite the hot arid temperatures, I would ascend to the rooftop, a flat patio type area, to contemplate and reflect on the state of the world and spend time in Bible reading and prayer with God. These prayers were intense, and I valued them as my consecration or refinement periods. The rooftop became my altar.

Coincidently, the minuets, Muslim temples, that strung out across the city were visible, and the imams' prayers could be heard echoing at regular times throughout the day. Whenever the prayer call rang out with a high-pitched tune over the city of Riyadh, I countered it with my own prayer, one of which I knew that God was hearing me on a very personal level.

At the end of my evening prayer time, just before heading downstairs to bed, I flicked a marble out into the desert night sky. Each marble represented my days away from home and signified that another day of being away from my family had passed. Before my deployment, I bought a couple bags of marbles, a total of 365, for just this occasion.

I lost sight of it almost immediately but would sometimes come across them lying in the sand while walking during the daylight hours the following days. They sparkled under the sunlight, catching my attention, but after a glance, I turned and left them there, lying in the sand. After all, that day was history. Yes, another day gone, thank God, and another day closer to going home and being with my family.

During the middle of my tour in Saudi Arabia, I was given the opportunity to travel to Dayton, Ohio, for a three-week class in contracting, one of which, contingency contracting, was preparing me for inevitable duty in Iraq. The trip to the United States entailed a flight on a Saudi Arabian airline with a stop in Paris, France.

A stocky young Arabian man dressed in Western clothing sat next to me and immediately began talking to me in English.

"They call me TJ. And you?"

"My name is Scott," I answered as we shook hands.

"What do you do in the military?"

Flashback to Berlin, I thought to myself.

"How did you know I was in the military?"

"Almost all of you Americans here have something to do with the military."

"I'm in army contracting."

"That's great! I'm the secretary for Prince Sultan of . . ."

I didn't understand the long name TJ was drawing through family lines. "Wow, you mean he is the son of the king?" I asked ignorantly.

"No, there are many, many princes here, and he is just one of them. He is very, very rich, though. I'm sure that if I talk to him, he would like to do business with the army, and he could provide anything you wanted."

"Well, I'm not that big in the decision-making process."

"But, surely, you know people. You must be an officer, maybe a major or lieutenant colonel?"

"Yes, a major."

"You have plenty of influence. Here is my card. Please call at any time. I'm going to Paris to be with him for a while. If you wanted to, you could stay with us. We have the whole upper two floors of a nice hotel in downtown Paris to ourselves and our friends. You would be most welcomed, of course."

I bet, I thought to myself as I could just visualize being in the presence of a prince surrounded by his harem. "Well, I am only passing through Paris on my way to the United States."

"You are coming back though, aren't you?"

How did he know that? "Yes, I'll be back."

"If you like, we can arrange for your return flight to come through Paris, where you can be our guest for a day or two before you go back to Riyadh."

This guy is good.

"Okay, we'll see. I'll check with my superiors."

"Great. Hey, want to see something funny? Watch! Once we get out of Saudi airspace, all the women on this plane will get up and go to the bathroom, and when they return to their seats, you won't recognize them because they take off their abayas and are dressed like any other Western women."

I chuckled at the thought, but later, when TJ got my attention with his elbow, I watched everything unfold just like he said it would. "Wow, what a difference!" I exclaimed audibly while thinking how sad it was for the women to be living under such an autocracy.

My two weeks in Ohio ended quickly, and I was fortunate enough to have Trena come up to stay with me for one of the weeks.

I had no intentions of traveling back through Paris despite a couple of phone calls from TJ while in Ohio.

When I arrived back to Eskan Village, the second order of business after sleeping was to report the incident to the military intelligence folks stationed there. Like in Berlin, a meeting was set up. I was to meet with TJ, at his request, in a hotel in Riyadh. TJ would not be alone; nor would I, for that matter. The MI folks sent another officer to travel with me.

My friend, Major Chip Dickens, gladly joined me on the trip downtown to meet the Saudis. We both knew to keep the conversation to business without commitments. Our role was to listen. The evening went well overall, with a good dinner buffet. Any follow-up to this meeting was quickly discarded, as I would be leaving for Balad, Iraq, within days.

Departure day arrived sooner than I really wanted it to come, but, like any good soldier, I was ready to comply. I would trade my luxurious suite for some unknown dwelling in northern Iraq. It took me a few days to get out of Saudi Arabia and Kuwait, but I was finally airborne on a sunny afternoon in October, heading into the war zone. After a nearly two-hour flight in a C-130, we began our approach into the Balad airfield.

At one point, I got up from my green nylon seat and walked over to the porthole to see the view outside.

What a barren wasteland. As far as I could see over the horizon, there was nothing but a brown surface, reminding me of photos that I have seen of the moon. I strapped myself back into the seat as we began our approach into Balad.

The sudden descent was not like any other I'd been through before. I could feel the plane making sharp turns while simultaneously diving downward. This corkscrew spin that the C-130 aircraft was performing as we spiraled down into the dry desert sands was a very common approach, an action taken to avoid the small-arms antiaircraft ground fire from the insurgents hidden in the vast farmlands surrounding the base.

CHAPTER 13

OPERATION IRAQI FREEDOM (OIF)
CAMP ANACONDA, BALAD, IRAQ
2003-2004

A trustworthy envoy brings healing.
—Proverbs 13:17(NLT)

The Balad Airbase was surrounded by stretches of barren desert with patches of verdant farmland. Groves of date palms pocketed the northern areas. Much farther to the north the desert reached into mountains as if trying to grasp new heights. Also to the north, toward Kirkuk, oil fields were clumped together with the derricks and refineries. The Tigris and the Euphrates rivers ran through most of the country from the northwest to the southeast. The area, once considered the Garden of Eden, appeared cursed to me.

The Iraqi Air Force once used Balad Airbase as one of its major installations. Now it consisted of vast military complexes, which were earth-covered bunkers—squalid, dilapidated and seemingly godforsaken dwellings.

The heat in the area easily reached 125 degrees Fahrenheit during the summer. During the wintry rainy season, the air was quite cold, damp, and miserable. The powdered, dusty sand turned into a muddy quagmire during the rainy season.

The plane touched down without incident, and we taxied to a stop. The whining sound of the C-130 tailgate slowly opened into the blast of warm air as our line of soldiers and civilians followed the lead off the ramp and onto the tarmac, where numerous aircraft,

C-5s, C-17s, Blackhawks, Chinooks, and other planes were either parked or moving for takeoff.

Our line proceeded past some red cones and crossed paths with another line of soldiers and civilians who appeared more eager to board the same plane we just departed and head back to Kuwait.

"Welcome to Mortaritasville!" somebody yelled amid the roar of aircraft.

I took note of the beleaguered faces on some of them, and most donned a variant style of sunglasses. I even had my own shades, none of which were army issued. It reminded me of my first purchase as an acquisition officer when I was in Saudi Arabia. It was for an order of protective sunglasses for the bomb-sniffing dogs. These were appropriately called "DOGGLES."

We continued our trek, which led to a place where our meager belongings, mostly duffle bags, were dumped in the dirt. We all began to make coordinating efforts to find a liaison or somebody who might know who and when we were coming.

Many on the plane found rides quickly; whereas, I fell into the category where nobody must have known that I was arriving. I was left to fend for myself from that point. After waiting a while with a meager hope that someone from the contracting office would come by looking for me, I gave up and bummed a ride from a deuce and a half, a two-and-a-half-ton cargo truck, loaded with soldiers.

"Do you know where the contracting office is?" I asked the driver as I threw my stuff in the back.

"Yes, sir, I know where it is. Hop in."

"Great. Thanks," I said while climbing up the back of the truck.

Winding down the narrow brown and dusty streets, the truck maneuvered through two traffic circles and came to an odd-shaped trailer that was actually two single units attached together.

"I appreciate the ride!" I yelled as I threw my bags over the drop-gate and watched them plunk onto the desert floor, sending a cloud of powdered dirt spraying upward.

"No problem, sir. Welcome to Balad!" the driver responded.

At least he didn't call it Mortaritaville.

I was anxious to finally get to my snivel gear, the remainder of my belongings that had been left on a pallet overnight in Kuwait because our original flight was delayed for twenty-four hours, a common occurrence.

I remembered that extra night in Kuwait, staying at Camp Wolf, as it was known then, standing in line while waiting to use the phone. A young female soldier who was watching me said, "Sir, do you ever get used to this?"

"Don't get too comfortable with war," I recall answering. My thoughts reverted back to our triumphal return from Desert Storm, when we were greeted with celebration bands and bleachers full of cheering crowds.

I knew then that we were not finished in the Middle East and that our children would have to go back and reengage in combat. This nightmarish thought was hauntingly made real to me that night with that young female soldier, who looked to be around the age of my own two kids.

Opening the door to the trailer as the officer in charge was walking out; I was greeted with, "Hey, are you the new guy we've been waiting for?" Major Harington asked.

"Probably so; Scott Meehan," I answered while extending my hand.

"Jeff Harrington. Welcome, we're glad you're here. Why don't I take you to your quarters first and show you where you'll be living, then we can go grab some lunch."

"Sounds good," I agreed, happy to be on the same wavelength in thought.

When Jeff showed me to my one-room trailer with a bathroom attached, I was rather impressed, since I'd had no idea what to expect short of tents.

"Here's how you get hot water," Jeff said as he held two exposed wires together that were dangling from the wall in an attached bathroom.

"*Zap-puff!*" was the sound emitting from the demonstrated attempt that coincided with sparks and smoke.

"Ahh, shhh . . . !" he began and then quickly spotted the Iraqi maintenance manager walking into the room. "Hey, Ali, I thought I told you to fix this? I need this fixed today! Today, Ali, you got that?"

"Yes, yes, we will fix it today; no worries."

"*Today!*" Jeff emphasized as if his bout with repairs was wearing thin on him.

"I take it that getting things fixed around here takes some time," I mentioned.

"You don't know the half of it," Jeff answered, shaking his head. Not wanting to explain and probably thinking that it would be best if I just saw everything for myself, Jeff said, "Let's go eat."

Lunch at the DFAC was crowded, but the hot chow tasted good. The only thing that spoiled an otherwise good lunch was when Jeff informed me about the mortar that landed just in front of the entrance two weeks before, killing a soldier.

After lunch, we headed back to the contracting trailer, where I was introduced to the rest of the team, then shown to my desk. On top was a pile of at least fifty contract folders that needed some kind of action completed.

"This is where you'll be sitting, and these are yours," Jeff told me, pointing to the stack of folders. "How much experience do you have in contracts?"

"None," I answered. "The army switched me from program management to contracting after sending me over here."

Jeff gave me a mixed look of aggravation and disbelief. He didn't have to say what he was probably thinking. Instead he said, "Well, I hope you're a fast learner."

I assured him that I was quite flexible and willing to learn.

My first night there at Anaconda, while sleeping in a half-way decent bed, I was awakened by what would become the all too familiar thundering sounds accompanied by ground-shaking vibrations. Not knowing at the time whether the source was incoming mortars or outgoing artillery, I rolled out of bed and felt for my flak jacket in the dark. Grabbing it, I laid it on top of me like a blanket, said a prayer, and went back to sleep. It was only three in the morning, and I was exhausted from all my travels.

The next morning, my first full day of work was slow because it was a Sunday. Fortunately, I had time and a willing volunteer in Captain Kathleen Jacobsen to help me with the cradle-to-grave contingency contracting process. Kathleen was quite knowledgeable and very patient; attributes that I really appreciated during this rapid transition. I'm not sure I would have known where to begin without her.

Based on the knowledge I received from Kathleen's tutoring, I was able to establish my own method for tracking the complex process that enabled me to adapt in a timely manner. Immediately afterward, I was initiating business relationships with the local Iraqi vendors. In time, I had gained the trust of these contractors as I looked at each one not only with compassion but as the future of Iraq itself.

"The quicker these guys can gain control of their country, the quicker we can get out of Dodge," I would say loud enough for everyone to hear. I figured that this was a positive concept and a good personal philosophy to embrace.

Although not exactly a kick-in-the-door frontline assignment, it was a critical position. I wasn't expecting to engage in any direct fire, but indirect fire such as rockets and mortar became a frequent occurrence.

I diligently worked long hours and did my best to make sure that the frontline troops had the best supplies, services, armor protection, and gear available. Anything and everything we could possibly think of to provide for the soldiers, both men and women—anything they desperately needed—I sought to procure from the local businesses.

Realizing that in order to make the whole process come together and be successful, I had to build a trusting relationship with the local Iraqis, fast! Soldiers' lives depended on getting what they needed, especially protective armor. I did not care if the Iraqis were Sunni, Shia, Kurds, or Christian.

Two months after establishing a decent rapport with the locals, one of the vendors approached me in a manner that displayed his more than usual nervousness. It was on the third of December.

"*Sabah-el-khayr*" (Good morning), I said, standing up as Whaleed* approached my desk like he always had.

"*Sabah-al-nor, Shlounak*" (Good morning. How are you?) We both placed our hands over our hearts at the same time while speaking.

"*Ani mumtaaz, al-hamdu li-llah, diamen*," I responded in haltering Arabic. Translated, it roughly meant, *I'm excellent, thanks be to God, always.* The contractors responded with lighthearted laughter any time I added the word, "diamen."

Our conversation continued in the customary manner at first. But then he cast a few glances from side to side and over his shoulder before he finally blurted out in a whisper, "We need to talk!"

"Okay, have a seat," I answered.

"No, not in here. Can we go outside?"

"I motioned with my head. "*Yella*" (Let's go.)

Whaleed had not been seeking business with me for very long, but he asked for me by name. Not too many Iraqis trusted other Iraqis if they weren't from the same background.

We walked a safe distance into an open field. His hands shook while lighting his cigarette.

"I have two cousins in Baghdad that have some information about Saddam's people." His glancing and quick puffs between words had my interest. "They don't trust Americans, so they won't talk. But I convinced them to talk to you. They want to talk with you. Can they come?"

I was both flattered and embarrassed at the same time. "Sure, Whaleed, I'll listen to them, but I will probably need them to talk to one of my friends." I remembered using that phrase carefully. "This sounds important."

"*Makuu mush-kila*" (No problem. I will bring them tomorrow!) Whaleed excitedly replied.

I shook his hand as if we had completed a deal and wished him a good trip back home.

"*Ma'assalama', Fii Mani Allah,*" or "Good-bye. God go with you."

That evening, I went to find Tony, one of my military intelligence buddies. He made some phone calls and arranged some of his folks, who were assigned to Camp Anaconda to be prepared for possible human intelligence in the next couple of days.

The following day, Whaleed approached me again with the same formalities, only this time he came with two other men alongside. Both looked to be in their late twenties or early thirties. All were dressed in Western-style clothing.

"*Assalam alakom,*" I began, meaning, "Peace be upon you," a generic formal greeting.

"*Alakom salaam*," they replied back, while placing their right hands over their hearts.

"Let's go outside," I told them.

Once again, walking a safe distance away from the crowd, the two Iraqis began telling a story in Arabic. Looking at Whaleed for the interpretation, I waited curiously.

"They said that they know where there is an important safe house in Baghdad, and Saddam's people are staying there," Whaleed said as one of the cousins interrupted in Arabic. "And even some relatives," Whaleed added.

"I see," I answered with renewed interest. "This is very important. Ask them if they would mind telling other soldiers if I introduced them."

Whaleed spoke to his cousins in Arabic. I saw that they were asking questions in response and then shrugged their shoulders, seemingly satisfied with Wahleed's answers.

"Okay, they will talk to these soldiers if you take them yourself."

"*Zein, yella*," (Good, come on), I told them and led them to the mayor's cell after contacting the military intelligence unit. Then I left them in their hands behind closed doors and went back to work on procuring much-needed products and services for the soldiers fighting the war.

Being consumed with my work, I almost forgot about the three Iraqis that I escorted to the mayor cell. Two hours later, they emerged from the long questioning and appeared at my desk, looking exhausted.

"*Yella*," was all I had to say as we all walked past the line of Iraqi vendors on our way to the open field behind our trailer.

"How did everything go?' I asked.

"*Coolish Zein*" (Very good), they answered.

"I want to thank you guys again for doing this. You have been a great help, I'm sure!"

They spoke excitedly in Arabic while Whaleed interpreted that they were very grateful, and they wish me safety and a prosperous time in Iraq.

"*Shukran!*" I replied.

We exchanged farewells as they departed with "*Theemall'ah*" (With God's protection).

As they walked away while trying to avoid the mudpuddles, I did not really know if it would be the last time I ever saw them. Turned out, it was.

Ten days later, on the night of the thirteenth of December, after the hustle and bustle of the contracting-business world was winding down, I went outside and peered up to the stars as I often did. Gunfire could usually be heard outside the perimeter at night, and tonight was no exception. Most often it was elements of the Fourth Infantry Division from Fort Carson, Colorado, that was involved in the firing in an effort to protect the compound.

Ready to sit down and catch a few minutes reprieve, I propped myself up against the side of the contracting office, a plain white metallic double trailer, and thought about the state of the war effort. I wondered, among many things, about the hunt for the "Ace of Spades."

Saddam Hussein was still in hiding. A lot of existing turmoil was attributed to the fact that somewhere he was calling the shots for the Sunni fighters we continued to encounter. At least this was everyone's thoughts at the time.

"Lord," I began, "please let somebody find this man, and maybe things will settle down some. If you can use me in this capacity in any way, please do so by any means. Only, help us get this guy."

Several miles to the north under the same moonless night from where I sat contemplating life's current events, approximately six hundred soldiers from the Fourth Infantry Division were in the process of conducting a raid in the small town of Ad Dawr.

A power outage, not uncommon, kept the entire area in complete darkness. Based on reliable and recent intelligence and accompanied by Special Forces who specialized in hunting down HVTs (high-valued targets), Fourth Infantry swept quickly through a farm compound near the banks of the Tigris River.

Bursting into a two-room hut inside a mud-walled compound, they found two beds, strewn with clothing, and a kitchen containing cans of spam meat and boxes of rotting oranges. Outside, between two farm houses surrounded by sheep pens, an old, worn-out rug covered in dirt laid flat on the ground.

One of the soldiers spotted the odd-looking, out of place, dirt-covered rug. He called for the commander, who promptly ordered a search. After knocking the dirt off the rug, the soldiers slowly pulled it back, revealing a thick piece of Styrofoam. Beneath the Styrofoam appeared to be a small hole. Sounds could be heard in the hole.

"Someone's in here!" the soldier yelled. Still yelling into the hole, he was ready to yank a grenade off of his vest and drop it down the hatch. Suddenly, uplifted hands appeared, one of them holding a pistol.

Kicking the weapon away from the slowly appearing hand, they quickly seized the man beginning to crawl out of the hole and jerked him out. The soldiers stared in disbelief! What they saw was a beleaguered old man with a scraggly gray and white beard.

"I am Saddam Hussein; I am the president of Iraq! I want to negotiate," the man said in English.

Standing there dumbfounded, one of the soldiers replied, "President Bush sends his regards."

Elated troops spread the word like a wildfire. Congratulatory remarks were being issued as if somebody had just won the Florida Lotto. After a few photos were taken, congratulations rendered, and jokes and laughter shared, the American soldiers were down to business.

They rapidly whisked Saddam Hussein to a waiting transport waiting across the field. Dark silhouetted figures of soldiers with glowing green eyes were spread across the landscape providing extraction security.

Days after Saddam's capture, when the behind-the-scenes stories emerged from numerous major media publications, I read that it was one of Saddam's close ties who told the American forces where he was hiding. I continued to read various articles and became astonished by some of the inside stories!

As I read, my eyes grew wider as the article talked about the informant who gave up Saddam Hussein. He was captured days before in a Baghdad safe house. The raid by the Americans came after receiving a tip from local sources shared with the Americans!

Wow! I guess building trusting relationships does go a long way after all.

Every day seemed to bring something new and exciting. One morning a young lieutenant came bursting into the office. "Sir, sir, look, we found one!"

The day finally came when an American soldier walked in with a piece of metal without the usual holes seen piercing through it. He placed the steel square down upon my desk and pointed to three chalk circles meticulously drawn on the sample. "We're in business!" he said, unable to contain his excitement.

I picked up the sample slowly and examined the front of the plate, the side of impact. I could clearly see three "dings" circled in chalk and marked as .9 mm, 7.62, or 5.56. But the story of the steel was told when I flipped it over. No dents, no protrusions, no dimples . . . the steel had withstood the small-arms fire test. We'd finally succeeded.

"Awesome!" I said, standing to shake his hand vigorously. "Where's the guy who has this metal?" I asked.

"He's here. I have him waiting outside. Do you want me to bring him in now?"

"Yes, bring him in now!" I repeated excitedly. "This is priority!"

Only weeks before, a battle captain had come into my office with a piece of metal and deep concern because he wanted to protect his soldiers.

"Sir, we're getting torn to pieces out there on the road. I'd like to get this metal installed on our Humvees, and we found a vendor who will do it. Can you do a contract with him?"

He handed me the metal, and I looked at it closely.

"Has it been tested?" I asked.

"Tested? How?"

"I mean, have you shot at this metal, and does it at least stop bullets?"

"Oh, no, sir, we haven't done that yet."

"Okay, let's do this. Take it downrange about twenty to twenty-five meters and shoot it up. Let me know how it goes. If it stops bullets, I'll sign him up."

I could see the frustration in his eyes.

"Do you have access to 7.62 rounds?" I asked.

"Yes, sir, we can get them. We'll do this right away."

A day later he came back with the piece of metal full of holes. Chuckling, he began, "I see what you mean, sir. We told the vendor that we couldn't use his metal."

"Good idea," I added.

This situation was desperate, though, and we needed a bright idea. There just had to be some local venders who could provide the method and means to retrofit these Hummers with protective armor.

I was able to obtain some Armox periodically, steel from Europe, but it was very expensive, scarce, and slow arriving. In fact, our primary Armox vendor had been shot and killed at one of our American checkpoints.

The need for something quick and abundant was crucial to keeping our men and women alive. It was time to embark on a new mission. These guys needed steel. Not just any steel, but steel that would at minimum stop small-arms fire like the AK-47s, 7.62 round.

The word on the street; *Major Meehan needs metal!* Protective armor for our troops was top priority! Firing 7.62 rounds from an AK-47 into the sample plates began. Test sample pieces arrived in droves. Venders came in proudly carrying the plates of steel, each with their own unique method of identification. Some plates were marked with chalk, others were painted bright colors, and others were with emblems and logos. There was even one sample that showed up round instead of square.

As soon as a sample made it to my office, it was sent out to the firing range, where soldiers belonging to Captains Moon, Kim, Price, and Stuckey would give it the official quality assurance inspection. In other words, they would blast away at the motionless plate of metal with all types of small-arms fire. Word soon got out, and other battle captains volunteered their troops for the quality assurance inspection.

Daily, the steel samples came in the front door and went out the back to the firing range. The soldiers would shoot them up, then bring them back . . . full of holes. Lack of quality was a foreseen problem.

These soldiers took great joy firing at the plates in the hope of discovering a solution, a plate that caused bullets to bounce. On any given day, I would look up from my desk to see one of them peering at me through a hole in a sample they had just shot. The plate would be tossed into the reject pile along with the many others. Then they would grab another freshly delivered sample and disappear out the back door, not ready to give up.

I could see in their eyes that determination to find the right stuff. It was with all of us. Anytime a vendor would see me, I always asked him if he worked with metal. *We're going to accomplish this mission and get back home alive!*

Finally, that day arrived! We found the vendor with the plate that stopped the rounds! We were ecstatic! The soldier brought in the two vendors. Neither of them spoke English. I needed our translator, Mohammed. Captain Stuckey also arrived after hearing the news that one of his soldiers conducted the successful test.

We went through the traditional introductions and then immediately got down to business. The negotiations were slow-going. Whenever I would ask a question, Mohammed translated to the vendor, who then began conversing in Arabic with his business partner before giving Mohammed his answer. Mohammed would then relay the conversation with me. This process went on awhile. Tell him this, ask him that, as the negotiations proceeded.

Much head bobbing and gesturing was involved, and the meeting was tedious but very necessary.

"How much of this steel do you have?" I would ask through Mohammed.

"We have a whole factory."

"That makes this same kind of steel?"

"Of course!"

Next I showed them the sketches I drew of the basic Humvee with the doors, floor, etc. that would need the armor. The vendors began calculating the dimensions. One version had nine pieces and another version had eleven.

"How much is it going to cost me per vehicle?"

More calculations but finally the cost, $600.

I looked at Mohammed and said, "Tell them that I need the price for the whole vehicle, not just for the door."

Mohammed spoke to them in Arabic, and they quickly nodded their approval and responded.

"That is the price for the whole vehicle," Mohammed said.

"For the whole vehicle?" I asked in astonishment.

"Eeeeeeee-yes!

"How fast can you deliver?"

"Delivery would begin at once."

The contract was signed, and the process began. Armor protection for our soldiers' transport vehicles was available immediately for production. Within weeks, the steel-plated Hummers and other transport trucks were on the road offering the American soldier a little sense of security.

The Iraqi contracting team spent time at a particular unit installing the armor onto the unit's vehicles. When they finished, they came back to find out what unit was next.

"His faithfulness will be your shield and rampart" (Psalm 91:4). Oh, how I loved reading the Psalms!

More and more, I found my days at Camp Anaconda to be busier than a Wal-Mart on Christmas Day. My typical day began at 0700. After cleaning up and putting on my desert camouflage uniform (DCUs), I would normally drive to the dining facility (DFAC) for breakfast and stop to pick up any soldier that happened to be walking along the road. I usually arrived to the contracting office around 0800. The local vendors began arriving at 0900.

There were constant business transactions taking place until I could fit in a lunch break sometime between 1230 and 1300. Then it was back to work until dinner. I took advantage during this time to squeeze in a workout at the gym, actually a tent, and shower prior to eating.

We were once ordered by combat medical stress teams to take time off. After dinner, it was back to work, usually until midnight. Often, these members from the combat medical stress staff would stop at the contracting trailer to check, discretely, on our mental state of mind.

Along with contingent acquisitions, a typical day included a barrage of mortars and rockets landing in the base with ground-shaking authority—and sometimes resulting in death.

That's how Camp Anaconda got its name, "Mortaritasville" or "Bombaconda."

Everybody learned to cope with this fact as well as other aspects of life that we encountered during the wintry rainy season. We learned to cope with sticky mud, leaky ceilings, brown water, burning garbage pits, swarms of flies, and rats. I once tried to save a rat. It was squealing from an area of glue that the pest control spread around my trailer. The critter was not only stuck to the floor, one of its legs was stuck to its body.

I proceeded to first meticulously remove the rat from the floor with a wet coat hanger and then, with the aid of a dust pan, walked it over to my shower. There, I ran the water on lukewarm temperatures, and then painstakingly began the task of removing the vermin's leg from its body. Ultimately, the operation was a success. However, in hindsight, I probably should have found a nice warm spot for it somewhere inside the room rather than releasing it outside in the cool evening.

Thick mud was also a problem during rainy season and stuck to everything like glue. There were also leaks in the living quarters and contracting office. To say nothing about the brown water, and the burning garbage pits causing bedtime hacks, which I found out later were from the garbage burn pits. Then there were the swarms of flies that gave us the feeling that we were in Egypt during the plague. In fact, at my desk, I was armed with my .9 mm Berretta pistol on one side and a fly swatter on the other.

The sand fleas, or sand flies, left gouging craters in human skin and potentially caused leishmaniasis. One day I devised a scheme to capture a sand flea intact. I emptied a can of Army-issued bug spray into my one-room trailer with the AC on full blast. Then I quickly shut the door behind me and left for the office, knowing that I wouldn't return until close to midnight.

When I arrived back to my room, I noticed that the walls in my attached bathroom were plastered with hundreds of these tiny critters, apparently blown by the air from the AC and stuck by the spray. I carefully scooped one onto a plain piece of white paper. Then I studied it with a magnifying glass that I had lying around to help me read small print in the dim lights.

What I saw astounded me. One might think that I had been in the desert too long, but I could see that the light lime-green monster was wearing what appeared to be a Kevlar helmet. Its nose was a sword. The teeth were equivalent to shark's teeth. Although the body was shaped somewhat like a seahorse, it had a scorpion tail! My conclusion was that these were normal insects at one time until they started harvesting in one of Saddam's biochemical pits.

These critters left such devastating bomb craters in the skin; there appeared to be no relief in sight. Well, nothing until I stumbled across a bottle of iodine-looking liquid that I thought was some sort of bathroom cleaner. The bottle was marked *Dextrol* and there was an emblem marked *Her Majesty's Service*.

Not knowing what it really was, I had nothing to lose and applied it to the areas of my skin that had already been attacked by these ungodly bugs. It worked! The razor-sharp bite marks went away almost overnight and were completely gone within forty-eight hours. I was amazed!

One of the perks I had as a contracting officer was to have a vehicle, Nissan SUV, assigned to me. I was able to get around the base, which was spread out in a five-mile radius. I took note of the soldiers walking back and forth along the main road and often stopped to offer them rides.

These soldiers here at Anaconda were special to me in a personal way. They were more than just American soldiers. They were our sons and daughters. Meeting their needs was the reason I was there in the first place. I viewed each young soldier as if he or she was my own son or daughter. My son was, in fact, at West Point during this time looking at a future with the US Army.

Thinking back on that moment with the young female trooper in Kuwait, I felt that I should have said more; that I could have done more. *But what?* I could have prayed with her. On a daily basis, I found myself trying to uplift the young lieutenants and enlisted soldiers even after hearing their stories and personal experiences of Iraq. The consensus was that Iraq was devoid of civic sensibility.

Villages were mostly hellholes of mud, sewage, and trash. Buildings were crumbling and graffiti-covered. Vast tracts of churned earth and garbage were everywhere, and with it the smell emitted. Many of the Iraqi people, however, had willing hearts, and they looked to us for their refuge. We needed to provide for their needs as well. Saddam Hussein sure hadn't.

One night after dinner I was on my way to one of the buildings containing phone service and access to long-distance calls. I made it a routine to stop by for the night to call home.

On the way I passed a troop bus stop where a lone soldier was sitting and waiting for the unpredictable bus. Without giving it much thought, I kept driving past the bus stop. When I turned the corner, I remembered that girl in Kuwait.

"What if that was my daughter sitting there?" I pondered. I turned my vehicle around and drove back to the stop where this young soldier was still sitting and waiting.

"Would you like a ride to your destination?" I asked.

"Yes, sir. Thanks," she said.

She needed to go several miles down to the south end of the base to her quarters. It was around eight thirty in the evening, and she was just getting off work. We shared some small talk along the way, and I tried cheering her up. She was quite pleased when I dropped her off in front of her living area, thanking me again and saying, "I had a hard day, and that ride lifted me up. Thanks again, sir."

Driving back toward the center of the base to make my phone call, I prayed, *Thanks Lord, for convicting me earlier and allowing me to meet a need.* I then remembered, as I turned a corner, that there was another bus stop just ahead.

Okay, Lord, you don't have to remind me this time. I'll pick up whoever is there. Sure enough, there was another young soldier sitting alone, waiting for a bus that may not even show.

"Would you like a ride?"

Gathering up his weapon and rucksack, the young man sauntered over and said, "Sure, sir. Thanks."

I asked how he was doing and did not expect his answer to be, "Not good, sir, I'm having a bad day." It appeared that he was doing all he could to keep from crying.

I wondered what was going on. "What's the matter?" I asked.

He then explained with a shaky voice how he just wanted to fit in with the guys, but they made fun of him and would not accept him.

Wow, I thought that the enemies who hated us lived outside the wire.

I let him continue to talk, and as we approached his destination, the base exchange, I knew I couldn't just leave him off without saying anything to him. I pulled over into the nearby parking lot and stopped the vehicle and starting talking to him. At the same time I asked God to quickly put the right encouraging words in my mouth.

Although I don't remember word for word what I said, I discovered several things. His name was Curt, and he was the same age as my son, Aaron. He went to an Assembly of God church in Maine and had been a Royal Ranger. I told him that I had been a Royal Ranger commander since 1987.

I tried encouraging him the best I could and let him know that he did not need to be somebody that he wasn't, and if he trusted in God the way he was taught as a Ranger, better things would unfold for him. I believed this myself!

I then informed him the procedures to seek counseling assistance, through the chain of command, and gave him my e-mail address and the building number where I worked and invited him to visit me. I shared my own testimony of how God dealt with me when I was his age and was first coming into the army.

"Curt, God heard your cry and felt your pain and sorrow because he sent me to pick you up, and that was no accident," I concluded.

Finally, after asking his permission, and unlike the girl in Kuwait standing in line, I did pray over him asking for his protection, blessing, and strength. Curt was scheduled to provide security the next day for a convoy traveling along the highways, the most dangerous job in Iraq at that time. As he slowly got out of my vehicle, he turned and smiled.

"Thank you, sir, for your encouragement and prayer and for the ride. I'll try and come see you in a couple of days."

I drove off heading back to my original destination to make my phone call feeling assured that my wife would understand why I was so late calling her.

Lord, there is no way in the world that this was a coincidence. Thank you so much for using me as an instrument to bring help to a young soldier. How many more of them are out there, thousands of miles away from home, fighting in a hostile, war-torn land, simply wanting to do their duty and get back home to those they love?

Indeed, our sons and daughters were here in Iraq and in Afghanistan. They still are. They are true heroes and deserve our prayers. My heart went out to Curt and the many young men and women like him. That night before I went to bed, I actually shed tears for them, praying for their very lives and that they would make it back home.

There was another such evening when I was looking for a place to sit down with my tray of food at the DFAC. I found a nice quiet spot at the end of a table. Two seats over to my left was another individual, a sergeant, quietly eating his dinner and seemingly deep in thought despite the constant drone of CNN in the background.

I opened with a casual greeting in which he responded accordingly. One exchange led to another as we began with small talk.

Now, as anyone who knows of the infinite knowledge and wisdom of God can attest, I was sure that this conversation would eventually lead to a much deeper level of communication than where it was currently.

Sergeant Kaminski talked about pragmatism versus idealism and mentioned to me that I should look up a poem by Rudyard Kipling, "The White Man's Burden," on a Google search. He equated the background of this writing—marines in the Philippines in the late 1800s—with our role today here in Iraq.

I assured him that I would. He then wanted to hear my views on everything that dealt with life in general. I took a deep breath between bites and then proceeded to unload. I told him about my faith in God and my reason for it, how with this faith, I did certain things and lived certain ways. I explained that the only way to experience this difference was for one to actually taste and see how good it really is.

He listened and then described what he thought to be attainable and what wasn't attainable. "What is for some isn't for others," he reasoned.

I agreed with him from a human perspective, but then added that there is one thing that is attainable for all mankind throughout the history of the world, and that is, God sent his Son, Jesus, to die for us all, and this gift of life was attainable for all who wish to have it.

"It's hard to compare faith with practicality," he said.

"You can call it coincidence, unusual, chance, or whatever you wish, but I'll call them miracles. Let me quickly share three of them with you."

I briefly shared with him about the trip home from Saudi Arabia after Desert Storm, my assignment to Orlando, and the miracle promotion after my dream. I added that all of these practical results were accomplished through my act of faithful prayer.

He smiled and said, "Yes, sir, some might call that chance, or the fact that the general in Florida found favor with you. Maybe it is because of the way you conduct yourself, and others are impressed."

"You're right," I said. "I've found that living by faith has incurred much more favor from many, including the one in whom I believe."

Sensing that our conversation had come to a conclusion, I arose from the table to don my flack vest and helmet.

"It was nice meeting and chatting with you, Sergeant Kaminski."

"Sir, thank you for sharing your views on life with me; they certainly leave one to think beyond just the relative matters."

"Sergeant Kaminski from . . . ?"

"New Jersey," he answered.

"If I don't see you again, stay safe here and remember, the love of God through Jesus is quite attainable for all mankind no matter where they live."

"I will, sir. You be safe also."

Hmmm, safety. Mortar and rockets landing on the base had become a daily occurrence. The indiscriminate targets often cost lives. One night, a rocket hit the rooftop of our new office, a concrete structure. It did not explode, but bounced off into an open field. Had we still been in the trailer, the rocket would have come through; whether or not it went off, it still would have caused considerable damage.

All of us were present, a bit shaken, but continuing with our usual late hours of completing the contract administrative tasks brought on by the numerous transactions during the day. I would have added this story to the others when talking to Sergeant Kaminski had it occurred prior to our conversation.

One morning, a month after the Fourth Infantry Division departed Iraq and was replaced by other units, the shadows descended from the treetops as the sun lifted over the east horizon just outside the north gate at Camp Anaconda.

None of the Iraqis waiting to enter the base had any reason to notice anything out of the ordinary. A private first class from the First Infantry Division stood in the newly built guard tower with his hands resting on top of his .50-caliber machine gun.

"Look at that quagmire," he said to the other soldier on guard. "Not all of them will get in today."

A massed array of pickup trucks, old-model Fords, and newer Toyota Land Cruisers all blended in with farm trucks as they sat still—like a sleeping snake. In uneven columns from the guard gate to the main road coming in from Highway 1, the Iraqi people, a mixture of Shia, Sunni, Kurds, and Christian, were used to long delays. On this day the delays seemed even longer than before.

The Iraqis came daily for a variety of reasons: work, medical attention, and the attempt for vendors to land a big contract with the American forces.

One particular blue Dodge held two bearded occupants. They were both dressed in the traditional Arab garb, called the Shemagh. Neither was smiling but fixed their glassy-eyed gaze straight ahead, oblivious to their surroundings.

It was as if they were strung out on some sort of potion or drug. Inside the trunk of the car were nine 155 mm artillery shells with wire of various colors wrapped around them. The shells were separated in threes. The wires led toward the front through an open area in the back seat and continued up to the lap of the passenger. In the hands of the passenger were a small mobile phone and a radio to where the wires ended.

Some of the other Iraqi drivers waiting to get into the base began getting testy and got out of their vehicles. Craning their necks, they attempted to discover the cause for their delay. Their normally displayed forlorn faces were unable to mask the current worsening situation.

On this morning, the expressed look was that of anxiety and contempt. The Iraqi drivers would complain bitterly, "Why won't the Americans let us enter this place? Here we are sitting in our own country."

New procedures from new commands usually took time transitioning into a particular desirable model. Base entrance procedures were no exception.

The two guards suddenly noticed unusual movement emerge from the line of cars. "Look!" one of them exclaimed. They both watched as the old blue jalopy started its engine and was trying to maneuver out of the packed line, forward.

"*Awgaf! Awgaf!*" one of the newly trained Iraqi guards shouted. He was checking the paperwork and identification of an elderly Iraqi gentleman when he noticed the vehicle approach. Dropping the contents from his hand and grabbing his assault rifle strapped over his shoulder, he shouted again. "*Awgaf te-ra ar-mee!*" (Stop, stop or I'll shoot.)

The sedan lurched into another gear and swung wildly out of the line trying to miss the SUV in front of it while speeding ahead toward the gate. The guards reacted immediately. With the .50-caliber bullets already fastened together in its feed tray, the American soldier aimed the gun in the direction of the rampaging vehicle and squeezed the trigger. He did so until the feed box was empty.

A volume of deadly pieces of armor streamed toward the oncoming car. The roar of the gun pierced the still, quiet morning air. Small puffs of smoke rose from the auto amid shattering glass. The car spun out of control and veered straight into the back of a truck full of vegetables.

Some of those who had gotten out of their own vehicles either jumped back into them or ran speedily in all directions away from the line.

Booom!

The thundering bang woke me up. I glanced at my watch. *Shades of Bogota.* Thick black smoke hovered over the area.

"Holy . . ." one of the guards began but was drowned out by all the screams and curses ringing out from all directions, both in English and Arabic.

Pieces of heavy debris and dirt rained down from the sky sounding like a hailstorm. An all-too-common chaotic scene, which often included body parts falling from the sky, began unfolding beneath the layer of dark black clouds forming from the explosive device manufactured for destruction. This suicide attempt was cut short by alert US Army guards.

After several minutes, the guards slowly rose from the ground and peered over the still-standing steel structure. They glared at each other, eyes widened, mouths opened but unable to speak, Kevlar helmet half-cocked to one side, a mixture of sweat and dirt streaming down their faces. Before them lay contorted metal of all sorts along with semidistinguishable body parts, which spread like a torn blanket smoldering in a field of carnage. Vehicles not obliterated looked as if a Mac truck had slammed into them.

Why so early? I thought to myself.

I valued the sleep I got from midnight to 0700. Swinging my legs out of the bed, I threw on my desert camouflaged trousers and uniform top. Then, quickening my pace, I continued to pull on my socks and desert boots. Finally standing up, I grabbed my armor protective flak vest and Kevlar helmet, skipped the usual look in the mirror, and headed to the concrete shelter just outside my room.

Had I made my usual stop in front of the bathroom mirror, I would have noticed the quickly aging features of a forty-six-year-old man, with a sharp nose, curved forehead containing fine, sandy-brown hair, and compassionate, yet piercing hazel eyes that seemed to penetrate through anyone looking into them. Beneath my eyes dark circles began to take form, revealing my weariness from long, extended hours.

I was pleased that so far I had not lost my hair to balding but still allowed the receding hairline and small tints of stray gray hairs to annoy me. I kept my hair cut short on the sides but long enough on top to run a comb through. Two creases, one on either side of my mouth, curved in an arch around the end of my lips from years of what I hope was nothing but pleasant smiles.

I walked out to the concrete bunker for shelter and waited with the rest of our contingency contracting team, which consisted of three officers and four enlisted soldiers. There, we would sit and wait until we heard the all-clear announcement over the loudspeaker followed by the all-clear siren.

When it finally came, all of the contracting team sauntered back to our trailers to begin preparations for yet another day in Iraq. As I headed back, I could see in the western sky, toward the airfield, a large plum of thick blackness caught up in a southerly wind current that was breaking up the peaceful blue sky. The source was coming from the north gate, two miles from my position.

Soon, the word spread from other soldiers in bunkers nearby that there was no mortar or rocket attack at all, as I had thought, but that there was a foiled car bomb attempt at that gate.

I had a few marbles left, meaning that my days in Iraq were numbered. I could see the light at the bottom of the jar! Finally, the much-awaited day arrived, May 19, 2004, with a manifest call at 1500. Just as predicted, the full day schedule was what I thought, hurry up and wait when it came to leaving Iraq and heading for home.

Going through all the motions to pack, getting manifested, waiting, going through customs, doing nothing—all had an underlining element of excited anticipation to it. I was going to go home!

There was plenty of time to reflect back on the year. It began in Riyadh, Saudi Arabia, and was now coming to a close in Balad, Iraq. There were times to weep and times to laugh. Besides all the heartaches that coincided with a separation and living in a war environment, our beloved dog, Rusky, had died while I was away.

I remember when Jacquie brought him home from the vet as a puppy shortly after Desert Storm, and he had traveled with us from Fort Bragg, North Carolina, to Fort Huachuca, Arizona, to Fort Polk, Louisiana, to Fort Bliss, Texas, and finally to Orlando. I walked into Jay Carr's-contracting officer office one day and said, "I'm thousands of miles away from home, my youngest just graduated, and my dog died."

"You need to see the chaplain," he replied without hesitation.

As I continued to reflect on various memories, I recalled the comical engineering event we had in our office. A stream of water looking like a solid sheet from a waterfall would come through the seam that was connecting the two singles to make the double trailer in our office.

We laid a line of buckets down the floor side-by-side catching the downpour while the maintenance guys worked on the fixes for nearly a month. To solve the problem, first they tried sealing the seam from one end to the other by putting large vice-grips up on the ceiling to hold together the beam. A large pole with a plunger at the end of it was mounted on a truck jack then cranked upward until the beam quit sagging.

When that didn't work, the workers went on the roof and caulked the seam from the outside with some strange-looking orange goop. That resulted in the drops of water still streaming through the seam mixed with hanging lines of orange, sticky, web-like strings that were attaching to everyone's uniforms.

The next thing we know, there's a team of guys drilling, hammering, sawing, and who knows what else on the roof, causing such a ruckus we couldn't even hear the person sitting next to us, making difficult negotiations all the more challenging. Jeff finally told them to knock it off after they tried to explain that they were creating a drainage canal on our roof.

Finally, an air force guy came by and offered us a survival tarp, which was fluorescent pink, to put on our roof. We decided that we had nothing to lose and had it installed on the roof, held down by concrete cinder blocks, making our trailer look like a giant birthday cake from a distance. It worked and was the final solution to our leaky roof.

It was during this whole process that we discovered our trailer wasn't grounded. During the frequent thunderstorms, the workers kept getting shocked when they went on the roof.

"All right, when I call your name, sound off with a loud "present," followed by the last four of your Social Security number (SSN)." That announcement broke the silence, and soldiers were jumping up from their slumber and excitedly gathering their belongings.

Name after name was called and finally, "Meehan!"

"Here, 1234!"*

I already had my rucksack on my back, and I hefted the remaining duffle bag over my shoulder and moved outside where the line began forming for the MP customs inspection. The sun seemed to be sinking rapidly below the desert floor.

After an hour or so, we eventually finished the rigorous customs process and were led out to a waiting area at the side of the tarmac. Then, at the signal, an airman led us out in two lines, exactly like when we arrived. As we walked toward the C-130 aircraft, its props cutting through the thick night air, the sound growing louder with each step, a new line of soldiers and civilians exited the aircraft.

They all wore the familiar apprehensive looks that we all had arriving in-country, wondering what would be in store for their journey ahead. Our lines passed close, and someone from our line yelled, "Welcome to Mortaritasville!"

The robotic motions necessary to process out of Iraq were complete but were shortly followed by the same humdrum procedures leaving Kuwait days later. Leaving Kuwait was more annoying because we had to put up with a few screaming MPs who thought that they were still at boot camp or took personal the fact that we were actually leaving a war zone while they were coming unglued in Kuwait.

Once aboard the chartered aircraft that would take me home, I exchanged greetings with the smiling flight attendant. Moving down the aisle, I scanned the seats for an empty one, away from the crowd. The jet's AC unit must have been running on high because there was a chill in the air that had the whole interior cold. I spotted the seat I wanted and proceeded to throw my gear into the overhead compartment. Others were sure to join me soon enough. Everybody wanted to go home. Why not? We did our time. Assuming we were all thinking on the same wavelength, none of us ever wanted to return to that godforsaken place again.

John Mayer's "Clarity" was playing over the intercom. How fitting.

> *This morning, there's a calm I can't explain*
> *By the time I recognize this moment, this moment will be gone.*

More weary soldiers continued to pile into the aircraft lugging their carry-on rucksacks. I reached for the headphones and placed them over my head. When I finally get to the other side, hours later, my wife of twenty-one years will be waiting for me! My son and daughter will be there also! I smiled at the thought. I can't wait to see them again. It was a long year. Too long.

Once the soldiers settled in, one of the flight attendants gave the safety instructions over the intercom while the plane moved slowly into position for takeoff. After a few idling minutes, we lurched forward and quickly gathered the speed needed for liftoff until we were airborne. Jethro Bodine once made the statement on *The Beverly Hillbillies*, "Uncle Jed, if this thing gets going any faster we will be flying off the ground." This revelation was during his first flight in a plane when he thought he was on a fast bus.

Airborne—yes, I remember it well. I earned those silver wings after completing five jumps at Fort Benning, Georgia, during the record-setting temperatures and miserable hot summer of 1980.

One of those jumps was a night jump. That is when, for a brief second or two, I thought life here on earth was finished for me. The night was darker than I thought it would be once I exited the aircraft. I was mesmerized by the night lights over the horizon. Suddenly, I noticed a canopy parachute looming large out of the corner of my left eye. I tucked myself into a tight body position and tugged hard at my right main risers to pull away from the approaching jumper, praying hard to avoid a midair collision.

Too late! I felt solid impact racing across my left side from lower leg to upper shoulder. I was now facing skyward with my feet in front of my nose. I'm rolling over his chute in midair! Just when I expected to see a new paradise, I noticed that my arms were joyfully jumping up and down on the ground, where I found myself lying safely on the ground.

I had just completed a dynamic point of landing fall (PLF) and did not realize it at the time. In the excitement of avoiding what I thought would be imminent contact, I did not even feel my feet hit the ground.

*Not real SSN.

Chapter 14

One More Mission
The Green Zone
Baghdad, Iraq
2005

A Tree in the Desert
No other way than the Son,
Life's true vine, the only one.
Lift me from the desert sand,
Like a palm tree I will stand.
Unshaken by wind and heat
I remain without defeat.

June 23, 2005, started out like any other morning while working at the palace in the Green Zone. The early-morning sun, already radiating unbearable heat, peaked over the eastern Mesopotamian horizon.

I was enjoying another session of physical training, a therapeutic start to my daily life, which began at 0500 with the sound of the alarm. I forcefully swung my feet over the side of the bed onto the always present brown, powdery-like sand covering the trailer floor.

The cloud emanating from my feet impacting against the floor usually produced a cough or two. I winced at the fine dust that I could taste as it lingered in the air. After about fifteen minutes, I was ready to walk to the gym, located at the north end of Saddam Hussein's old presidential palace.

The palace was now the most prominent structure in what was dubbed the Green Zone, so named because outside, in the rest of Baghdad, or the Red Zone, one met with an increased risk of horrific violence. Early in the morning I began a ritual that included weight lifting in the gym, a run around the palace perimeter, and swimming laps in Saddam's pool.

On the morning of the twenty-third my swim was interrupted by thunderous explosions. The blasts came from the south, just across the river. I not only heard the violent sounds, but could also feel the concussion. My first thought was, *Lord, please protect the team; I pray that none of them are hurt.*

Nine of my thirteen employees came from that direction when they arrived to the Green Zone for work. It was my task to train them in the basic administration of contracts. Together, we supported the Joint Contracting Command-Iraq. Our job was to audit and then close out Developmental Funds of Iraq (DFI) contracts. These contracts dealt with the money given to Saddam from the UN to feed his people, known as oil-for-food.

This money never was used to benefit the Iraqi people, since Saddam held it all for his personal use. The American soldiers found it all stored away in the palace when they arrived in the spring of 2003. It was used for various projects during the Iraq reconstruction. Now, the new provisional government wanted what was left, and we needed to track it.

I permitted all of the workers to vary their arrival times, within a reasonable window, so that their chances of arriving to work safely were enhanced. It was a known fact that coming to work was a risky business for Iraqis who dared work for the infidels.

The thirteen employees who worked for me represented the moderate, educated, and the progressive future of their country. They were college educated and could speak, read, and write English fluently. One of them, Tara,* also knew Spanish. I used her as my primary translator to track down Iraqi contractors who had done business with coalition forces in the past.

I halted my swim sooner than planned and headed immediately back to my trailer to get cleaned, refreshed, and ready for the day. My first order of business would be to account for all Iraqi personnel and make sure that my whole team had made it to work unharmed.

Usually I worried about them as if they were my own children even though three of them were my age or older. I felt responsible for them, and, at times, the younger ones acted just like my own.

The reports came from across the Tigris River, indicating that chaos was the order of the day (Al-Salhy 2005). On one sidewalk, a young boy screamed as he sat next to his mangled bike, his left leg missing below the knee. An Iraqi man noticed him and went over to comfort him. Scooping him up in his arms, he carried the child to a passing military police Humvee, where soldiers grabbed him and quickly administered life-saving first aid.

Yelling, screaming, crying, horns blaring, whistles blowing, and sirens wailing were all part of the typical sounds after such an act of devastation. Shutters from surrounding stores lay on the sidewalk from the force of the blast along with other debris, shattered glass, concrete slabs, charred vegetables, fruit, and, of course, automobiles (Al-Salhy 2005).

I did not see the devastation, but there isn't much difference between the results from a bomb exploding in Baghdad and one detonating in Balad or Bogota.

The few trees present were now toppled, scattering leaves among the ashes. Whoever was responsible either died as a suicidal maniac along with his vehicle or simply slipped over the Jadriya Bridge with the rest of the traffic and melded into the Qadisiya District of western Baghdad.

Since Prime Minister Ibrahim Al Jaafari had come to power only two months before, more than 1,240 people had been killed in similar fashion. Others were simply shot to death after being kidnapped and tortured, solely because of their particular style of belief in God.

Those mighty Islamic warriors—just like them to carry out their dastardly, heroic deeds against kids on bikes armed with a dangerous bag of fruit or candy. No doubt, the only god who could be pleased with such great bravado is Satan himself.

I met up with most of my team during breakfast in the palace, a place where the feeding frenzy vigorously took place three times a day. The dining areas were surrounded by spiral marbled stairways and glittering chandeliers.

The large, grandiose meals drew folks from all over the world: Russia, Australia, Nepal, United Kingdom, South Africa, etc. The variety of behaviors, appearances, and styles of those who conducted business at the temporary American Embassy was astounding.

"Thank God you are all safe," I said to five of the girls who were just sitting down with their trays. "I'll get my food and join you," I continued.

"Hurry!" Lyna said, "We have much to discuss."

Lyna was the outspoken one, always cracking jokes in Arabic, causing the rest of them to roar with laughter. I often wondered if they were at my expense, but after the laughter died down, she would always explain the joke. It was never directed at me, or so she said.

She was shorter than Tara, about five feet five, and kept her reddish hair shoulder length. Her eyes were a light brown, and every time I saw her, she was smiling, often mischievously.

"Let me have one of your cigarettes," Saif, one of the employees, said to Lyna one day.

Giving him a look of disdain, she asked, "Does your mommy know you smoke? Would she approve?"

The table erupted in laughter, and even more so when he responded to her with something in Arabic that did not sound so nice. The two of them jokingly went after each other in such fashion. I had somehow miraculously orchestrated a young team of Iraqis who, despite their variety of backgrounds, got along like family members most of the time.

Only once did I need to play the part of a referee when some volatile verbal exchange between two of them nearly came to blows. The issue was eventually ironed out.

It was not uncommon for them to have a Sunni father and a Shi'ite mother or vice versa, and when I would ask, "Are you Sunni or Shi'ite?" The response was always, "We're Muslim."

Devouring breakfast was one of the team's favorite events of the day along with their constant stashing of fruit to take back to their desks and ultimately home. This pilfering soon resulted in a change in DFAC (dining facility) policy.

"We all want to stay with you tonight," Lyna told me as the rest of them laughed.

"Huh?" I responded.

"Yes, you heard me. None of us can sleep anymore because there is still no power, and it is *coolish haarr* (very hot) even at night."

I used this term once before to describe how hot I was feeling one day, and all the ladies erupted in laughter. Apparently, there are different meanings to the same word when describing the weather outside and describing myself.

"You still don't have any power?"

"No, none of us do, and this place, Iraq, is not good anymore. We want to leave," Dalia chipped in.

"None of you have any power in your homes?" I asked again incredulously.

"No. We have to go to the rooftop and pour water on the sheets so we can stay cool while we try to sleep," Lyna stated.

I was dumbfounded and didn't know what to say. Here were Iraqis helping Americans find two hundred million unaccounted-for dollars, much of which had already been turned over to the provisional government, saying that they didn't have electricity to meet their basic needs even after two years!

"Where's all the money going?" I asked them.

"In the politicians' pockets and out of the country," Lyna said as the rest of them laughed but only in disgust. "You are lucky because you don't have such corruption in your country."

"Who said that we don't?"

"You just don't; we know this."

"Well, we do, sort of," I quipped, "but it is legalized. In our country the Mafia has given way to special interests groups and lobbyist."

"What's that?"

"Never mind. Long story, and besides, that's just my opinion."

"Oh."

At this point, the team began arguing heatedly with each other in Arabic. Then, just when their discussions appeared to reach a boiling point, and I might need to intervene, the room was filled with sudden laughter.

Just like them, I thought. *So full of optimism and life despite living in such hellish conditions.*

Overall, I was very pleased with this assembled team. Marwan, the youngest member of the team, lived in a state of fascination of his surroundings and was a true "wannabe" American. He seemed so juvenile in many ways but quite innocent. I gave him the benefit of a doubt in contrast to looking on him as a spy when he wandered the palace in awe. He just didn't fit the part of a spy.

One day, while sitting at my desk and mulling over the statistics, Lyna leaned over and asked me to join her as she went on her cigarette break. Although I never smoked, I would sometimes take the opportunity to join her on her breaks to find out what was on her mind.

"Okay; give me five minutes," I answered.

"All right, I'll be at my desk when you're ready."

Only five months before, while working at the palace, I had turned in my retirement paperwork, which had made it all the way to the desk of the retirement branch manager. Mr. Walker was ready to stamp his approval on it when I called him and asked him to put it on hold for six months.

Physically speaking, the Defense Contract Management Agency-Orlando, where I was currently assigned, needed to send someone overseas for six months TDY. Spiritually speaking, I felt that God wanted me to go back to Iraq one more time.

"You won't have to go if I approve these, you know," Mr. Walker had told me.

"Yes, I know, but, I feel that I need to, and that's why I'm asking if you could lay this request to the side temporarily."

"Six months. Okay, call me when you come back and make your decision."

"I will."

I had given this decision much agonizing thought and prayer and felt that it was what God wanted me to do. Trena fully supported me in this. So after coming home from Iraq in May 2004, and fully believing that I would never return, I left for Baghdad in March 2005.

I once vowed that I would never go back to Iraq, but I went anyway, knowing that God's plan and purpose is always bigger than my own limited view of the world.

Walking over to Lyna, I said, "*Yella!*"

Lyna jumped up, laughing with the rest of them, who continued their contract administration tasks.

Sitting down at a picnic table under a tree, Lyna began, "How long have you and your wife been married?"

Surprised by the question, I answered, "Almost twenty-four years now. Why?"

"I can tell that you love her."

"Yes, of course. Very much."

"I don't think my husband loves me," Lyna continued after inhaling on the white lipstick-stained stick hanging between her fingers.

"Why don't you think he does? I'm sure he loves you."

"Well, he has girlfriends," she said abruptly.

"Oh."

"You don't have girlfriends, do you?"

"No, I don't, not like what you mean."

"I didn't think so."

Silence.

"Why not?"

I wasn't too sure where Lyna was going with this, so I answered, "First of all, because like I said, I love my wife. Secondly, we both love God and have faith in him."

"You read the Bible, yes?"

"Yes I do, often."

"Can you get me one that's easy to read in English?"

"I sure can," I responded, "as soon as we go back inside."

"Good, thank you."

I was always careful not to preach about my spiritual beliefs to my Muslim employees.

I reasoned that the best thing I could do as a Christian was to simply act like one—a man of integrity, respect, compassion, and love.

Another day in the palace had come and gone. The team and I continued to meticulously uncover hundreds of millions of dollars.

This huge sum of currency never left Saddam's palace; that is, not until the American forces came in and took over.

The money was distributed throughout various commands to use as part of rebuilding the Iraqi infrastructure, though a large portion was used for projects that would sustain a longer US presence and safer environment. The JCC-I command assumed we wouldn't account for all of the money but wanted us to account for as much as possible.

The team I was allowed to put together was in the middle of auditing nearly two thousand contracts and successfully closing them out in the proper format. We at DCMA were ourselves audited by the Special Inspector General of Iraq Reconstruction (SIGIR). The amount of money we discovered to have been delegated for major projects yet never spent because the projects just didn't happen, was mind-boggling.

One evening an old friend, Dewayne Jira, who I knew from Fort Bragg in 1992, came by for a chat and drink. He had already retired and was there as a contractor.

"You know, Dewayne, it's not working."

"What's not working?"

"Democracy . . . here."

He just looked at me waiting for me to go on.

"Nope, and I don't believe that it ever will," I continued.

"Why do you say that?"

"Because we're trying to push democracy on these people while leaving out a vital aspect of democracy."

"Which is?"

"Christianity," I said, matter-of-factly. "It's nearly taboo in our own country now, so no one equates it with the success of our democratic system."

"What do you mean?"

"Well, while it's true that our Constitution and democratic system are ingenuous, I believe that what made the United States great was an early culture infused with Christian values and principles. Because we've moved away from those principles, the Muslims see how ungodly we are and probably now equate democracy with heresy."

"So, what you're saying is, Iraq has a good reason to mistrust democracy?"

"Maybe the way it is now."

We talked about many other things and then parted ways. I walked over to the pool area, where crowds had already gathered in droves, and where the music was playing loudly from the boom box. I took a seat on one of the lounge chairs and thought about my future service.

I knew that my chances to make lieutenant colonel were a ways off. Despite receiving a Bronze Star for my time in Balad, Iraq, I did not receive stellar rating. My report card did not have the check in the box marked, Above Center Mass (ACM), the highest rating an officer could receive on his/her Officer Evaluation Report (OER).

A week after giving Lyna the Bible, I asked her if she'd had a chance to read it.

"No, not yet," she replied.

"*Leish laah*?" (Why not?) I asked.

After a chuckle, she explained, "Because my father picked it up and is reading it, and he won't put it down."

"Oh, wow! What does he think of it?" I asked.

"He is finding great peace."

"*Zein!*" (Good!) I said with a smile.

* Not her real name.

Chapter 15

The End of the Journey

The medevac choppers descended, leaving blue skies behind and entering the ever-present brown, powdery haze that hovered over the scorched land. The swirling blades kicked up everything on the surface, making the air even denser.

Then, one after another, they landed onto the helipad located behind the street from the Combat Support Hospital (CSH). Military medical personnel waited as they stood near two small, green ultralight all-terrain vehicles called Gators, each with litters stretched across the back. Poles with intravenous (IV) solution bags were mounted at the ends.

I watched as the medical team grabbed the litters and walked toward the aircraft. Then, out came the combat-wounded soldiers lying lifelessly on the green canvas as they were being transferred to the Gators. From the top of the seven-story Freedom Building, I prayed silently for the injured and the relatives of the deceased as I stood watching the unfolding events below.

Behind me on the rooftop patio, laughter and music blared as a birthday party was being celebrated for one of the Iraqi workers. She turned eighteen. It was common here in the Green Zone to witness celebration and tragedy mingled together. It was all around us on a daily basis. Human life balanced on an uncertain threshold.

The flurry of activity to save lives continued to transpire below me; a festival of sorts was being celebrated behind me; and just ahead over the horizon amid the Baghdad skyline, another plum of black smoke rose sharply into the hazy sky from yet another suicide bomb blast.

Slowly, I joined the crowd to be a part of the birthday celebration. Soldiers and locals were eating, drinking, and dancing to traditional Iraqi songs mixed with a blend of the contemporary popular sounds. The food was traditional Iraqi, and there was plenty of it. I was going to miss my team of Iraqis. I admired their personal struggles of survival.

As my time in Baghdad approached the end, so too did my military career. Trena and I discussed the matter of retirement and I, more than she, was convinced that it was time to retire. This tour, along with the other one I had in Balad, began to wear on me.

Many preparations were made to make the final transitions and to turn over my duties to the incoming naval officer slotted to replace me.

I wanted to make sure that I personally showed my appreciation to and thanked the Iraqi team I had hired six months earlier that helped me audit contracts for the Joint Contracting Command-Iraq. Together, we were able to find more than $250 million that otherwise would have been lost.

I selected certain days to meet with each of the workers I had employed. I wanted them to know how, in their own unique way, they served and how much I appreciated their efforts. I handed each one of them a special gift in the process.

They received a letter of recommendation with the appropriate military signatures that would ensure them an opportunity to gain freedom from their current state and a chance to live in America if the need should ever arise.*

My one-on-one talks with them turned out to be harder on me than I thought. "I swear, we had the greatest times of our lives with you," one of them would tell me.

"You have something in your heart more precious than diamonds and shinier than gold. I think your heart is filled with love. That's what makes you so special. We will never forget you." Hana's words sank deeply. I didn't know what to say or how to respond, and I felt the emotion well up inside of me, fighting to hold back tears.

My heart went out to my team. I also thought back to the vendors I had gotten to know in Balad. I came up with a short and simple poem one evening when the eldest gentleman working for me had his bike stolen. He expressed in painful detail how much he relied on that bike for transportation. As he did so, tears welled up in his eyes. I felt so much compassion then. Fortunately, we were able to get enough funds together to get him a brand new bike.

One night while having my devotions, I began to think, *Lord, did I accomplish your purpose here? Is this why you sent me, for these people? You needed me to plant the seed?*

His answer was immediate, just like it had been when I was on the train in East Berlin. I turned to the passage that read, "Restrain your voice from weeping and your eyes from tears for you shall see the reward of your work" (Jeremiah 31:16 NIV).

The final two weeks for me were the most difficult. One employee came to me looking for a temporary place to live. She had received word that she was on the insurgents' hit list because she was working for us.

"Four people with ties to Americans were murdered in my neighborhood in the past two weeks," she told me. Although we were able to offer her a place to stay temporarily, she settled for a paid leave of absence to find a new house.

My replacement soon arrived, and I gave him a brief rundown and then introduced him to the team. This happened the day after I found out that the team had drafted a letter signed by all of them and had given it to my commander asking that I would be able to extend my stay longer.

After introducing my replacement, I took time to express my gratitude for their letter but said that I had made the decision to retire from the army. It was difficult to finish everything I had to say, so I stopped abruptly and said, "Let's go; we have a function to attend."

Later in the evening following dinner, and long after I'd thought everyone had gone home for the day, Marwan was waiting for me; he wanted to have a talk. We sat down, and I asked him what was on his mind. He told me that when I couldn't finish my statement earlier everyone knew why, and he asked me not to do that again.

"Why, is it a sign of weakness, and I'd lose all respect?"

"No, Major, it shows all of us even more how much you care for us and love us. It is getting too hard for all to know that you are leaving."

As expected, I had a hard time responding, so I remained silent. Then he added, "Why are you so different from any other American any of us have ever known?"

As one might imagine, I had many thoughts swirling through my head, wondering what he really meant by his statement. "You really want to know?" I asked him.

"Yes, of course!"

"In 1980, I was going through some very tough Special Forces training, and I made it. The problem was that I became self-reliant and arrogant. Then a moment came when God spoke to me, and I listened. He reminded me of his Son, Jesus, who died for everyone in the world because he loved us all. This is why I act differently than others," I told him.

He just looked at me. It was his turn to hold back the tears, and when he finally was able to speak, he just placed his hand on my shoulder and said, "Thank you, Major. I'll not forget this." Then he left for the weekend.

Days later I overheard another major tell my replacement, "They won't forget him; they love him to death."

I don't know if I'd go that far in my assessment of their feelings toward me, but the words struck me nonetheless. I sure know of a great friend who actually did love me to death. In fact, he loved us all to death, so that we could live.

In three different ceremonies recognizing my departure, I said in each one, "I am concluding my twenty-five-year military career with probably the most gratifying year of them all. What we are doing for the Iraqis here in their country is beyond description. It has been extremely rewarding to be part of the forming of liberty for a nation and to help in the freeing of their people from tyranny and oppression."

I knew the battle in Iraq was not just a battle between flesh and blood. There were powerful forces at war in what was once considered the Garden of Eden. The mission was still not complete and would only be completed when the Messiah returns. Until then, there will always be a great need for spiritual warriors to accomplish his purpose.

On my last day at the Green Zone, I stood in a picture with the team, those who came on their day off. We walked together to LZ (landing zone) Washington. Four of the local male employees walked with me to LZ Washington, carrying my baggage.

I will always remember Bassam, Saif, Marwan, and "Big Dog"** as good friends. We said our final good-byes. Like with the Russian years before, we exchanged hugs. Then, before I boarded the Blackhawk, Marwan handed me a note. It read:

Dear Scott,

We are really proud of you, proud of your
Friendship, courage, confidence and love that you gave us.

You are more than a leader for us,
For each one of us you were father, brother and friend.
We are grateful for each day with you.

Thank you for your kindness, friendship, and love.
Thank you for all those times you stood by us.
Thank you for all the truth that you made us see.

Thank you for all the love we found in you.
Thank you for every single memory which has become part
   of us.
We wish you joy, happiness and faith. We love you.

I folded it up nicely and placed it in my carry bag with the intention of securing it in my Bible next to the passage, "Clearly you are an epistle of Christ . . . written not with ink but by the Spirit of the living God" (2 Corinthians 3:3).

I recalled a moment in 2002 when I once asked a former Muslim lady at my home church in Orlando, "What was the primary factor that led to your decision to accept Jesus Christ as Lord?" Her answer was simple. "The love I saw in those who had Jesus."

While sitting and waiting for the C-130 at BIAP (Baghdad International Airport), I asked another soldier to take my picture. This was to be the last picture taken of me wearing the uniform of the United States Army.

* Three years after I departed my team in Baghdad, Dalia, one of those who worked for me, sought asylum and was allowed to come to the United States as long as our family agreed to sponsor her. This we did, and she lived with us for several months before moving onward with her husband, who came later.

** The brave man we all knew as "Big Dog" was gunned down in the streets of Baghdad six years later.

As a contingency contracting officer at LSA Anaconda, Balad, Iraq (2003)

A local contractor installing tested armor protection for our troops (2003)

Landing at Air Base Balad (2003)

Eighty-Second soldiers guard the north gate at Camp Anaconda (2003)

"Big Dog"

A short visit to the palace in the Green Zone by the secretary of state (2005)

The last photo of me in uniform as I prepare to leave Baghdad.
I retired two months later (2005)

CHAPTER 16

FINAL WORD
BAGHDAD, IRAQ—2006-2007

As the Blackhawk continued to aim toward the Baghdad streets below, I thought, *Not another Blackhawk down!*

Life wasn't at all what I was expecting it to be after I retired. The initial job that I had lined up with SIGIR fell through. For three months I was on a roller-coaster ride of emotions and thoughts, wondering who and what I was. I kept thinking, *I should be doing something now, but what?*

At one point I dug through the book cabinet and found what I was looking for. It was the book titled *From Army Green to Corporate Gray*. I flipped through the pages searching for something useful. Going over the assessment section, which included the categories of what I did best, enjoyed the least, and where I excelled, I spent a good amount of time building a matrix to determine what I wanted to be after the army.

Finally I reached the point where the assessment period just had to come to a close. It seemed I was getting nowhere. This was a period when I felt like I was standing on the edge of the earth and could not see over the horizon. I went for evening walks, confided in my best friend and wife, Trena, and prayed.

Trena, as always, was a great source of support and inspiration. I always knew that I made one of the best decisions of my whole career when I left the Special Forces when I did. Her presence now made the whole process less devastating than my current perceptions.

One evening, I received a call from a recruiting company. They desperately needed someone with my qualifications to return to Iraq. "Are you willing to go?"

I looked over at Trena. My heart said no. She looked at me. I asked her what she thought about the idea. We concluded that accepting the interview at least wouldn't hurt anything. "Let's just see how God opens doors."

"Okay, I'll accept an interview."

When I arrived in Washington, everything went smoothly. I met several people within the command structure, including the president, who owned half of the business. His sister owned the other half, in an office complex in Los Angeles, California. I was also to meet the prime contractor, SY Coleman.

I read through their mission statement and verbally noted how much it matched my resume. Without formally telling me that I was hired, they wanted me to schedule a trip to Los Angeles to complete the contract and fill out the insurance paperwork.

After just a week I flew out to LA and met the other part of the team. The paperwork shuffle went without a hitch because of the competent administration. When my two days of administrative work were complete, the other owner and sister called everyone available into her office. What happened next was astounding!

"Scott, can you pray for our team here, and afterward we'll all pray over you and your safe travels and work in Iraq."

I was more than happy to oblige.

Leaving home and Trena was not easy, and I never really got used to it. Had she not supported this new job offer, I would never have accepted it.

My new responsibilities, after twenty-five years in the army, were to handle the payroll and the contracts of at least fifty Iraqi advisors living throughout Iraq. This meant taking control of the financial accountability for the northern sector of the Advisor Task Force mission.

In order to accomplish my task, I would have to fly long and odd hours by either a Blackhawk or a Chinook to a variety of places across Iraq's northern region. The cities traveled to included Tal'afar, Mosul, Kirkuk, Baqouba, and Baghdad.

It was during these trips when I discovered that all coalition aircraft regularly released its flares whenever the pilot felt the threat of danger from a signal that has locked onto the aircraft. So on the night we were descending rapidly into the streets of Baghdad, the pilot was simply taking evasive action. There would be no imminent danger for this night. Life continued.

Ten months later, during the same route, a Blackhawk was shot down before reaching its destination to Baqouba. All twelve passengers and crew lost their lives.

I reached my destination, the headquarters for operations at the D-main (Division main HQ) of the 101st Airborne Division at Camp Speicher. Part of this division, and located a few miles down the road, was the 3/187th Rakkasan Brigade.

They had the distinction of being the force that did considerable damage to the Iraqi army during Desert Storm. They were known to have flown 175 miles into Iraqi territory in the largest air assault operation ever recorded.

Making numerous flights with an undisclosed amount of cash in my rucksack throughout Iraq was part of my new job. Cash payments and accountability were made at each stop. A typical flight on a CH-47 Chinook would take me on a long, excruciating journey lasting four and half hours just to travel 120 miles. This was due to the numerous other stops in remote locations spread throughout northern Iraq.

The usual view for me from the air included various shades of black, which provided the scenic desert floor, sprinkled with the rising curved terrain features of small peaks in the north. The foreground consisted of stoic silhouettes of soldiers trying to sleep the best way possible. Wearing their body-armored flak vests containing the twenty-five-pound bulletproof steel plates and their Kevlar helmets; they sat against the mesh seats.

The loud drone of the rotors made it necessary to wear earplugs. The door gunner looked like something out of a science fiction movie with his aviator's helmet equipped with night vision goggles (NVGs), or the Nods. He sat draped over the edge of the ramp while attached to a harness secured back in the fuselage. His eyes glowed with an ominous fluorescent green from the Nods. Arrival times to destinations usually ranged from midnight to 0400.

Then the task of finding a place to bed down for the night ensued. Whenever I traveled to Mosul, I would meet with the American liaison the day following my arrival. On this particular morning in Mosul and after a very short night of sleep, I went on the mission to obtain some hot coffee.

On the way back to the terminal, I asked one sullen soldier standing guard how he was doing.

"A lot better than that girl in there." He pointed to a small trailer placed in a makeshift area called Mortuary Affairs.

"What happened?" I asked sympathetically.

Replying in a disgusted tone he said, "A suicide bomber drove his vehicle into her truck right outside the gate. She was twenty-three," he added.

Almost Jacquie's age, I thought.

Shortly thereafter, I met with the American manager there in Mosul. He was distinguished by his long, flowing locks and facial hair. Most of the managers, retired Army SF operators, had their own unique style of appearance, which did not resemble anything military. Typically, their demeanor was calm, their attitudes were full of confidence, and, by the nature of their experience, their heads were full of wisdom.

Although I never enjoyed the hassle associated with the traveling, I thoroughly enjoyed talking with Rich and discussing philosophies of life. We normally concluded business with dinner before he drove me back to the terminal for my flight back.

Another three—to four-hour flight back in another Chinook to my home base awaited me. When he dropped me off and I headed toward the waiting area, I noticed that everyone was standing and looking out in the direction of the tarmac. I walked over to the barriers to see what was taking place.

A C-130 four-engine turbo-propelled cargo plane was sitting there with its tail dropped toward a formation of soldiers. The back of the plane was lit up by headlights from a variety of caterpillars and other military vehicles. They were conducting a ramp ceremony, the protocol for a fallen soldier being honored during a memorial service.

After the ceremony, the draped casket is taken aboard and flown to the soldier's home. A long formation of soldiers stood quietly while the sinking sun cast its glow on the airstrip. In the background, the distinct wailing of the call to prayer broke the silence as it echoed from the local mosques.

Once the casket was loaded on board the aircraft and out of sight, the soldiers marched away. The rest of us, who witnessed the service, turned back to the terminal and went about our business awaiting outgoing flights. The waits varied in time; there was no set schedule.

After waiting for hours, two Chinooks appeared with their lights flashing. Their destination? Camp Speicher! Hooray! As we boarded the aircraft, I couldn't help but notice that the young sergeant I sat next to looked like he was Aaron's age or younger. He was guarding a PUC (person under control) or detainee. On the other side of him was another sergeant looking just as young.

The Iraqi man sitting between them wore the traditional long white robe called a *dishdasha* and dust-covered sandals as his footwear. Tied around his head and covering his eyes was a pressure dressing normally used for direct pressure on bleeding wounds. Every soldier carries one with him or her. In this case it was used as a makeshift blindfold. His hands were cuffed in the often used flex cuffs. I didn't bother to ask what his offense was. It was pointless. I wouldn't have been able to hear his reply anyway.

The return flight had fewer stops and only took three hours. I arrived back to the base at 0330 and fortunately had my Toyota Prado waiting for me, which I used to transport another weary traveler, like me, back to his CHU (container housing unit). The HESCO concertina surrounding the CHUs loomed ahead.

The HESCO sandbox, used as a protective barrier, was a prefabricated, multicellular system made of galvanized steel weld mesh and lined with nonwoven polypropylene geotextile. The units were usually held together with joining pins and filled with sand.

On one of my last flight missions there, I traveled to Baqouba, or FOB (forward operating base) Warhorse, on the way to Baghdad. Standing on a lonely, dark landing zone (LZ), I first heard, and then spotted the silhouettes of two CH-47 Chinook helicopters. After they set down, blades still twirling and sending gusts of wind and sand in all directions, I lowered my head and approached the rear of the second chopper. The rear door gunner met me.

"Are you going to Baghdad?" I asked.

He nodded his head over his shoulder as a sign indicating that I should come on inside.

The aircraft was full, but the right front door gunner waved his hand toward the front and pointed to a seat by the door. I unstrapped my large rucksack and dropped it at my feet in front of me alongside the pile of the rest of the gear. Sweat poured down both sides of my face, and I could taste the salt on my lips.

While sitting toward the front of the aircraft, I had a nice view outside the door gunner's side opening. I saw the dark silhouette of the second helicopter at our one o'clock position. I drifted in and out of sleep for a period of time until I noticed the glittering lights of Baghdad in the distance as we approached the city's southeastern outskirts.

Boom! Like a Fourth of July firework, the chopper I was watching lit up with flames shooting back from both sides, turning the black surroundings to bright orange. Thank God, it was only releasing its flares to misdirect whatever locked onto it.

The view of the firework display was quickly blocked by our door gunner, who jumped up to man his gun while the other two (left front and rear) did the same. With a lurch, the helicopter shot forward and out into the vast darkness, on course to Camp Liberty.

My heart was back on course as well. It was another moment of evasive maneuvers and business as usual for this part of the world.

We made a quick turnaround stop at Camp Liberty and then headed to Camp Speicher. The Chinook was nearly empty. The gunner was one awesome dude, though. He fished out a cold Gatorade from his ice chest and handed it to me—amazingly refreshing.

During my year working as a contractor I was able to travel home on four different occasions: my son Aaron's college graduation, a Colombian reunion, my and Trena's twenty-fifth wedding anniversary, and Christmas.

While I was home I took advantage of making an appointment with my doctor for a physical examination. I was feeling a bit stressed while in Iraq and a little restless. I was told that my cholesterol was too high, and I needed medication. This was not really what I wanted to hear.

On my way back to Camp Speicher, I made out an eight-week schedule that included a workout regime at the gym, planned meals with certain foods, and, of course, my ITWG. my acronym for intimate time with God—basically, meditation.

As always, our flight from the United States to Iraq included a stop in Kuwait and an overnight or two at Ali Al-Salem. I was at Ali Al-Salem on a Sunday morning, so I attended the service at the chapel.

The chaplain was very eager to give away a variety of literature. I saw a table full of spiritual reading material. One of these was the small pocket Gideon's New Testament (with Psalms and Proverbs) that brought back the memory of that evening before my first jump at airborne school. I took it along with me.

When I arrived back to Speicher, I stayed diligent with both my spiritual and physical schedule. I also did a lot of driving between places in my brand-new vehicle, and I constantly passed soldiers walking back and forth to their workplaces and the DFAC or CHUs.

Normally, it was 120 degrees Fahrenheit with the "windchill" factor of 130 F. Gusty winds whipped up the brown, powdery dust, turning the air brown. I made the decision to regularly stop and offer a group of soldiers a ride to their destination. Though usually short, I could tell by their overwhelmingly positive response that even a little was appreciated.

Sadly, I was told by many that I was the only one who would stop, as they watched vehicle after vehicle pass them by, leaving them in a trail of dust. I was happy to be there to help, especially since I was blessed to have a vehicle.

The only part that I didn't like about the short trips was that they were too short. I could not engage in deep conversation with any of them and had little chance to share my faith.

One evening before going to bed, I asked God for an opportunity to engage with someone who needed to hear about him. Shortly thereafter, I was scheduled to fly to Baqouba but discovered that the flight had been canceled. My idea for this extra time was to take advantage of going to the gym. I was going to lick this high cholesterol.

On my way to my parked vehicle, a young sergeant stopped me and said, "Excuse me, sir, do you have a vehicle?"

"Yes, I do. Where do you need to go?"

"I'm not really sure because I've just arrived here, but someone told me that I needed to go near the air terminal."

"That's almost to the other side of the base. Hop in," I said. "I'm sure we'll find it."

He expressed his gratitude, and, after assuring him that it was no problem at all, we began our "journey."

Our first stop turned out to be the wrong place. Likewise, the second, third, fourth, and fifth stops were all incorrect. Each of these stops were quite a distance apart. I also stopped on several instances to ask for directions for Sergeant Dominique Amarral.

Finally, after more than an hour of searching, we were able to find the location to his unit, and we both breathed a sigh of relief. Numerous times during our search he apologized for the trouble he got me into and told me over and over that I could just let him off to fend for himself.

I wouldn't hear of it and assured him that everything was fine. "In fact," I told him, "I was just praying to God for such an opportunity, and for you to ask me for a ride was not an accident."

I went on to share about my faith in God and gave a few personal testimonies. When I brought him back to the tent where he would be staying, I handed him the Gideon's New Testament pocket Bible I had picked up in Kuwait. I also inserted my business card in the back section explaining the plan of salvation. He shook my hand several times before departing and zipped his new Bible into his uniform shirt pocket.

As for my workout at the gym, it didn't happen, but I had a good spiritual session.

Two verses stood out to me. "Neither he who plants nor he who waters is anything, but only God, who makes things grow" (1 Corinthians 3:7 NLT), and "We are Christ's ambassadors, as though God were making his appeal through us" (2 Corinthians 5:20 NLT).

On my last morning at Camp Speicher, I stood in the sand with no structures around me to notice the hazy sunrise just over the horizon in the east. Simultaneously, the white full moon appeared to be the same size as it was just sinking below the horizon in the west.

That evening, just before boarding a Blackhawk for Baghdad, this same phenomenal sight appeared in reverse. The sun was bright orange as it dropped rapidly to the horizon in the west while the hazy, reddish full moon appeared over the horizon in the east. I was amazed!

When I had the privilege of going home for our twenty-fifth wedding anniversary in October, Trena and I enjoyed a cruise. This one-week cruise took us to the western Caribbean and included stops at the Grand Cayman Islands, Belize, Costa Maya, and Cozumel. From the moment we launched ship, I was in a surreal world far, far away from the desolation in Iraq. There were continual cool breezes instead of the furnace blasts of the desert heat. "He rides on the wings of the wind" (Psalm 104:3 NLT).

Amazing to me was that water was everywhere I turned, in place of the dust and barren land as far as the eye could see. Various shades of blue stretched out to the horizon! The land, well, there was green. Lots of it. Everywhere!

And the sun. Though a bright yellow, it did not seem to cast its rays on the inhabitants of earth with fierce anger like it did in the desert. I was taking in the array of colors, so often taken for granted. It was refreshing. Gone were the brown water, brown landscape, brown streets, and brown sky.

Being with my best friend and sharing together some good that life had to offer, such as quiet, relaxing moments of reminiscing, eating food that appeared to be prepared for royalty, and doing a variety of fun activities, instilled in me the feeling that I had to be in paradise. Indeed, for one week I was.

The stark contrast between the two environments caused me to think of heaven and hell. One, a place where fire produces torment and agony, the other a place where the streets are made of gold, the crystal clear river of Life flows from the throne of God, the trees of life yield their fruit, and the Lord himself is our light—a place where there will be rest and no more tears.

I had no doubts. The wasteland of Iraq is as real as the tropical paradise islands of the Caribbean. The contrast is stark, yet both exist. This is also true for heaven and hell. Luke 23 describes the criminal hanging on the cross next to Jesus who said to him, "Jesus, remember me."

Jesus Christ, the Son of God replied, "I tell you the truth, today you will be with me in paradise."

Trena and I stood on the lido deck, watching the waves of the gulf and feeling the cool sea breeze as the sun dipped below the surface. "I'm getting closer to my home."—Grand Funk Railroad.

**With Trena celebrating our twenty-fifth wedding anniversary
with a Caribbean cruise (2006)**

References

Al-Salhy, S. 2005. "Iraq blasts kill at least 23, scores wounded." Retrieved from http://www.newsdaily.com/stories/tre75m57t-us-iraq-violence/

Matthews, C. 2006. "9/11 mystery: What was Atta doing on 9/10?" Retrieved from *http://www.msnbc.msn.com/id/14686192/ns/ msnbc_tv—hardball_with_chris_matthews/*

Meehan, S.A. 2004. "Sons and daughters." Retrieved from *http:// www.pe.ag.org/Articles2004/4727_My_turn.cfm*